ABAP in S/4 Hana

By Mark Anderson

Table of Contents

Introduction 7
    Structure of the Book 8
    Conclusion 9

Chapter 1: ABAP in Eclipse 11
  1. Installation 12
      1.1   Download and Install Eclipse 12
      1.2   Install the ABAP Development Tools for SAP NetWeaver (ADT) 13
      1.3   Connecting Eclipse to a Backend SAP System 15
  2. Features 16
      2.1   Create Domains 16
      2.2   Creating Data Elements 20
      2.3   Creating Structures 22
      2.4   Creating Classes 27
      2.5   Deleting Unused Variables 31
      2.6   Searching for Objects 31
      2.7   Formatting ABAP Source Code 33
      2.8   Using Where-used List 34
      2.9   Navigating to SAP GUI 36
  3. Summary 37

Chapter 2: New ABAP 7.4 and 7.5 Language Features 39
  1. New Language Features 39
      1.1   Inline Declarations 39
      1.2   Internal Tables 42
      1.3   String Processing 44
      1.4   Calling functions 49
      1.5   CONVersion Operator 50
      1.6   CASTing Operator 51
      1.7   VALUE Operator 52

1.8	FOR operator	54
1.9	Reduction operator REDUCE	56
1.10	Conditional operators COND	57
1.11	Conditional operators SWITCH	59
1.12	Corresponding Operator	60

2. Summary 61

Chapter 3: Core Data Services 63

1. What Is S/4 Hana? 63
2. ABAP Programming model in SAP S/4 HANA 63
   - 2.1 Introduction 63
3. Code Pushdown 65
4. Core Data Services (CDS) 65
   - 4.1 CDS Views: A Step-by-Step Approach 67
   - 4.2 CDS Views 77
5. Summary 88

Chapter 4: ODATA 89

1. What is OData? 89
   - 1.1 OData Architecture 89
2. Gateway Service development 90
6. Summary 104

Chapter 5: Business Object Processing Framework 105

1. Introduction to BOPF 105
   - 1.1 Business object Meta model 106
   - 1.2 Nodes 107
   - 1.3 BOPF Actions 109
   - 1.4 BOPF Validations 111
   - 1.5 BOPF Determinations 113
2. Creating BOPF Object from CDS views 115
3. Summary 115

Chapter 6: Exercise - Building a draft-enabled business object 117

1. Scenario 118

    1.1   Create a Base table for BP header and Identification data 119

    1.2   Create the Interface View for the base tables 121

    1.3   Create the Transactional Processing View 124

    1.4   Create the Consumption View for the User Interface..143

    1.5   Create OData service..147

    1.6   Transactional Processing..157

2. Summary..164

Conclusion 165

Introduction

Over the last four decades SAP technology has evolved at a great speed.

SAP systems now touch 77% of the world's transactions and are the leading source of operational data like financials, customer transactions, supply chain, human resources, Insurance etc.

The first SAP Application was for Accounting (R/1 system), followed by SAP R/2 system towards the end of 1970s, which was based on mainframe computing.

In 1992, SAP developed the client/server application we all know as R/3. Several PCs could be used to connect with the one or more application instances which would process the data on one or more instances of the database.

In the first three decades, SAP was primarily focused in building robust Application software and used 3rd party databases e.g. Oracle, DB2 etc. Furthermore, many customers wanted to use latest UI technology. Hence SAP software found itself sandwiched between 3rd party software providing UI and Database.

The journey of evolution continued, and SAP made great strides in the areas of Development tools, User Interfaces, Business logic and Database technology.

To maintain a lead in the market SAP then introduced S/4 Hana as its own Database on 3rd February 2015 at the New York Stock Exchange. The event introduced cloud and on-premise editions, and launched the on-premise edition.

With the SAP technology changing so much over the years, the developers across the world found it difficult to adapt to it.

Although all the SAP developers would love to use the new features but most of the programmers who would benefit from it found it difficult to understand and implement the new technologies in Client implementations.

The purpose of this book is to enable the inquisitive ABAP developers to adapt to the new ABAP programming model. This book will help them be aware of the SAP-delivered improvements and it also provides Exercises which will guide them in a way that they can start implementing requirement using the newer technologies.

Structure of the Book

The book is divided into six chapters. Each chapter focuses on a specific function and provides examples relating to it. Chapter 1 starts with the installation of the Eclipse and the next chapters guide the reader through the journey of creating new Application based on S/4 Hana architecture. Chapter 6 covers an end-to-end exercise and helps in bringing together the concepts covered in this book.

Chapter 1: ABAP in Eclipse

Chapter 1 describes how to install and update the front-end components of ABAP Development Tools (ADT) for SAP ABAP on HANA. This is important as SAP has shifted its focus to using Eclipse as its development environment. Hence an SAP developer must become familiar and start using Eclipse IDE for all its development.

Chapter 2: New ABAP 7.4 and 7.5 Language Features

In this chapter, you are introduced to new language features of ABAP 7.4 and 7.5 and focus on the large number of new features. This includes new commands and constructs.

Chapter 3: Core Data Services

This chapter introduces Code Data Services (CDS) Views and explains how the code pushdown works wonder for the performance of the applications. It also explains the best practices and the tools recommended to be used for developing applications in the S/4 Hana world.

Chapter 4: OData

This chapter explains how you can expose backend data via OData services. It explains the OData architecture and includes an example of how you can create a new OData project and expose data to the outside world.

Chapter 5: Business Object Programming Framework

This chapter introduces Business Object Processing Framework. This chapter does not aim to cover BOPF as it is a big topic which should be dealt separately. This chapter only focusses on some aspects which help in the development in S/4 Hana world.

Chapter 6: Exercise - Building a draft-enabled business object

This chapter starts with the introduction of Draft-Enabled Business Object and provides a step-by-step exercise on creation of CDS Views and exposing the data via OData interfaces.

Conclusion

Reading this book will provide an overall end-to-end view on how to develop a new application in the S/4 Hana. The topics discussed will reinforce your current knowledge and help you develop your skills in unknown areas.

Chapter 1: ABAP in Eclipse

ABAP's development environment has gone through many improvements over the years. When I first started coding in ABAP, it almost felt like I was in the stone age. Prior to working in ABAP, I worked for almost 2 years in web technologies and then adapting to the ABAP development environment was a bit of a challenge. It required getting used to filling forms (instead of coding) to create objects. The settings were quite complex, and you had to have a good understanding of the available settings.

No matter how hard I tried, there was always something new to learn in ABAP and it took me quite a bit of a time to understand that I had to unlearn at the same pace as I was learning new things. There were changes to the way we programmed, and the good practices somehow became a not so good practice over time. Be it using Classes instead of Function modules, ALV instead of List views, or the new ABAP debugger. I must accept that I resisted using the new debugger simply because I had got used to the old one and was not mentally prepared to unlearn the best tool I had at my disposal. It took me a few days of vacation and a strong heart to try the new debugger. Now after having used the new one for almost 12 years I am afraid that this might be taken away from me very soon! I am sure a similar kind of anxiety is in the minds of other ABAP developers and we are afraid that we must adapt to the new way of coding in ABAP.

When I was introduced to ABAP development in Eclipse, I could hardly sleep for a few days. There were many questions which I tried to answer – will the ABAP development environment become obsolete? What about the best Transport Organizer in the world? Do I now have to check-in and check-out the code? Etc.

I have learnt over the years that the best way to overcome fear is to face it. Hence, I started exploring the new features and the Eclipse development environment for ABAP. I must accept that it was not easy but now I am convinced that this is the way forward. The eclipse development environment does not take away any features but add a lot of tools and capabilities which improve the development experience. In fact, many new objects (e.g. Core data services) can only be created and edited using Eclipse.

Eclipse is an integrated development environment (IDE) used in computer programming, and is the most widely used Java IDE. It contains a base workspace and an extensible plug-in system for customizing the environment. ABAP development in Eclipse requires ABAP plug-ins.

In this chapter we would go through the installation process and familiarize with the environment. This will set the right base for the rest of the chapters in this book.

1. Installation

Following steps are involved for setting up the Eclipse development environment.

- Download and Install Eclipse
- Download and Install the Eclipse Plugin for ABAP development
- Connect the Eclipse to the Backend SAP system.

1.1 Download and Install Eclipse

To download and install Eclipse, please follow the instruction in the below link:

https://tools.hana.ondemand.com/#abap

You could also install Eclipse directly from eclipse.org but it is best to follow the detailed instructions in the provided link.

The link also provides detailed information on Prerequisites of Installation and Installation procedure.

```
SAP Development Tools

HOME  ABAP  BW  CLOUD  CLOUD INTEGRATION  HANA  IDM  ML FOUNDATION  MOBILE  SAPUI5
```

Prerequisites

Component	Prerequisite
Eclipse Platform	Photon (4.8)
Operating System	• Windows 7/8/10, or • Apple Mac OS X 10.11, Universal 64-Bit, or
Java Runtime	JRE version 1.8, 32-Bit or 64-Bit
SAP GUI	• For Windows OS: SAP GUI for Windows 7.50 • For Apple Mac or Linux OS: SAP GUI for Java 7.50 SAP GUI is not required to work with SAP Cloud Platform ABAP Environment.
Microsoft VC Runtime	For Windows OS: DLLs VS2010 for communication with the back-end system is required NOTE: Install either the x86 or the x64 variant, accordingly to your 32- or 64-Bit Eclipse installation

Figure 1: SAP Development Tools

1.2 Install the ABAP Development Tools for SAP NetWeaver (ADT)

Once the Eclipse has been installed, the ABAP Development Plug-ins can be installed from the Eclipse menu bar, select: Help > Install New Software menu option.

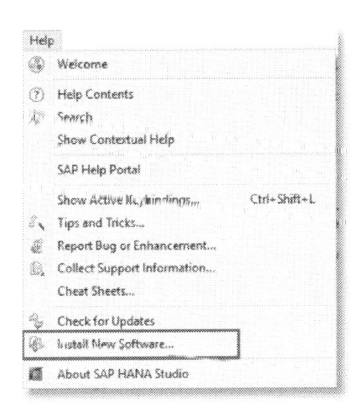

Figure 2: Install New Software

In the dialog box add the URL https://tools.hana.ondemand.com/neon (e.g. for Eclipse Neon 4.6)

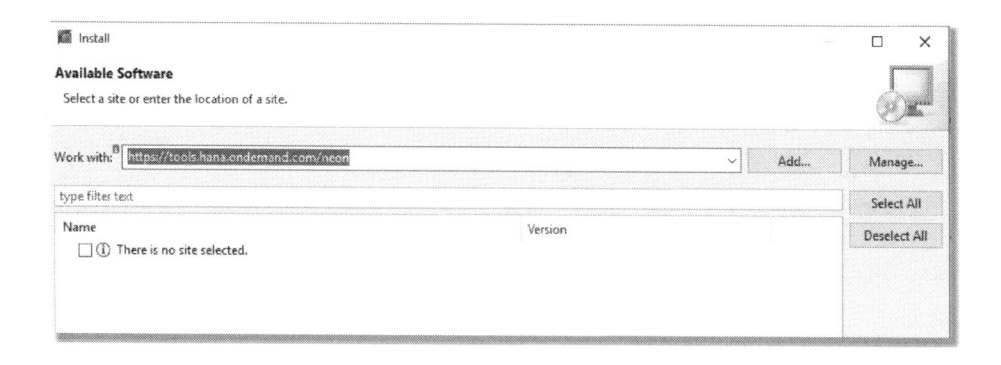

Figure 3: Available Software

Press Enter to display the available features. Select ABAP Development Tools for SAP NetWeaver and click Next.

On the next wizard page, you get an overview of the features to be installed. Click Next.

Confirm the license agreements and click Finish to start the installation

You can switch to the ABAP perspective by clicking the **Open Perspective** button or using the menu: **Window > Open Perspective**.

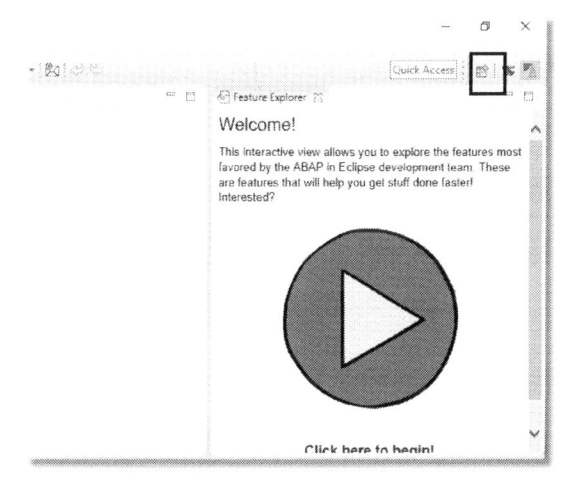

Figure 4: Open Perspective

1.3 Connecting Eclipse to a Backend SAP System

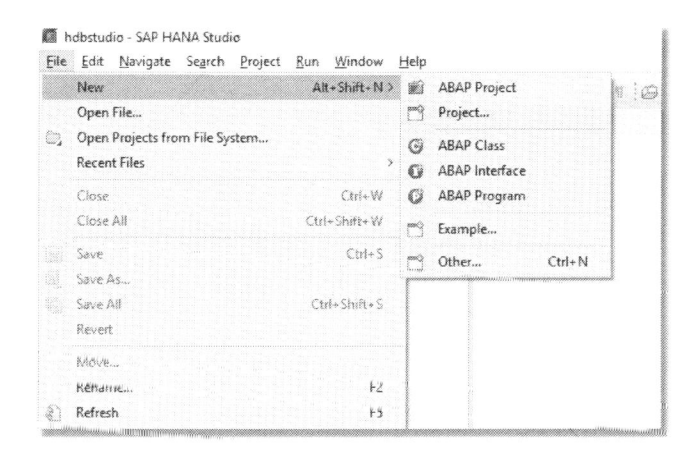

Figure 5: Create New ABAP Project

Once the Eclipse and ABAP Development Plug-ins are installed, we are ready to connect to a SAP backend system. To connect, choose the menu path - File –> New -> ABAP Project.

All the systems from your SAP Logon pad are listed in the next dialog box. Choose and provide the credentials with the client information to login and fetch the technical development objects.

Now the system is added on the left panel and this can now be expanded to navigate to the development package. It is also possible to add the development package as a Favorite package.

2. Features

In this section we will familiarize ourselves with the ABAP development in Eclipse. Most of us would have extensive experience creating ABAP objects in SE80, but it becomes important to be able to use Eclipse with equal ease. With that in mind, we will go through the process of creation of a few objects. The focus here is to understand how we can create the objects in Eclipse rather than the artifact themselves.

This chapter also describes how we execute some simple tasks like navigating to SAP GUI, Formatting the code etc.

Section 2.1 to 2.4 explains how you can create ABAP Artifacts using Eclipse and Section 2.5 to 2.9 explain some frequently used features.

2.1 Create Domains

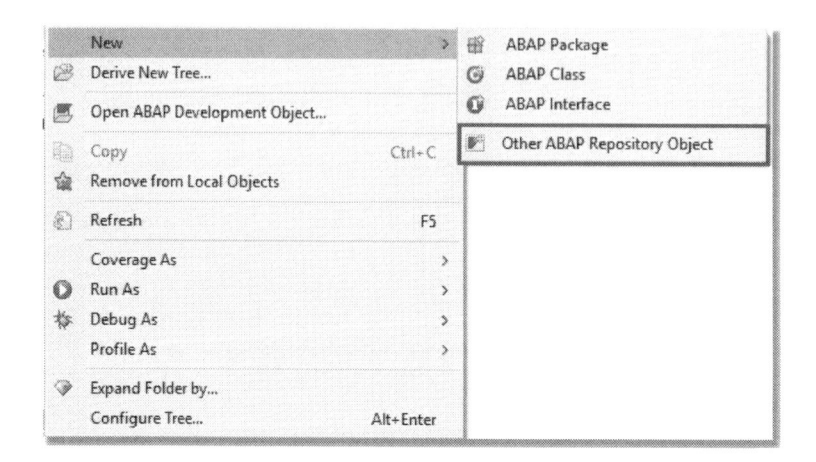

Figure 6: Create ABAP Repository Object

The DDIC objects can be created by right-clicking on the package and selecting New -> Other ABAP Repository Object, as shown in Figure 6.

This opens a dialog which can be used to create all kinds of ABAP artifacts.

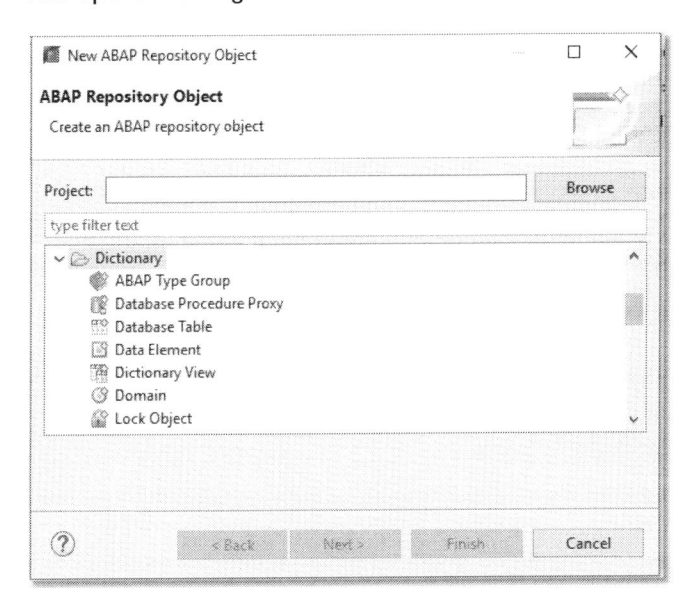

Figure 7: Create Dictionary Object

Select Domain and click on Next.

The next dialog requires the name of the Domain and the short text.

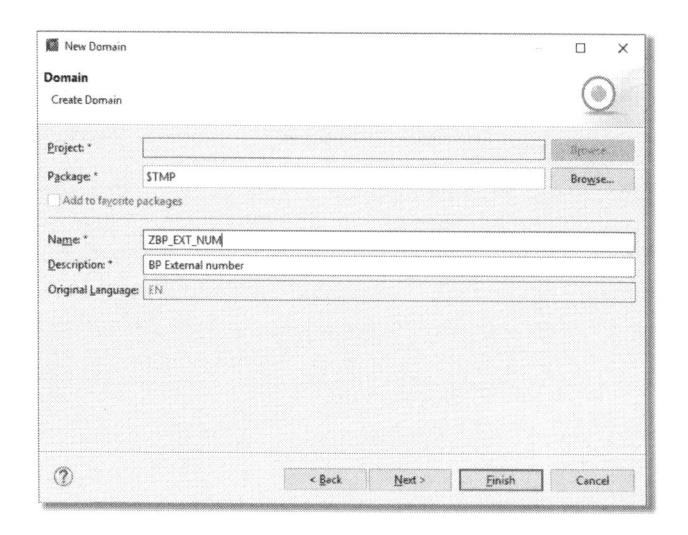

Figure 8: Create Domain

At this point, the system asks for the Transport Request. If the objects are created as a local object (in our case) then the TR is not required.

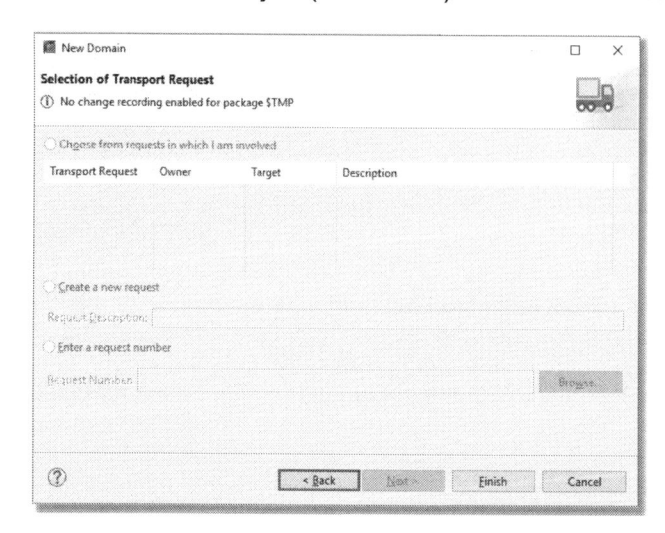

Figure 9: Select Transport Request

The next dialog provides a Form to fill the details of the Domain. It is interesting to note that all the relevant fields are in one screen. Hence, instead of navigating between different tabs (which often led to forgetting to fill a few attributes) the user can fill all the required information in one screen. This reduces the chance of missing out on entering important attributes and the constant struggle of finding the correct attributes in the different tabs is gone.

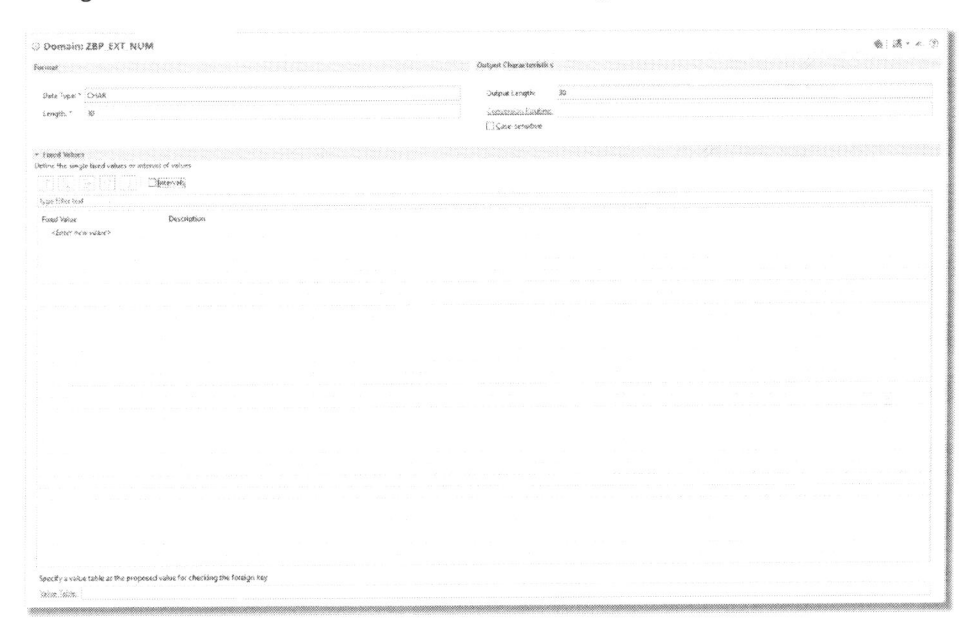

Figure 10: Enter Domain details

The Screen also provides more options on the right-top corner. The options allow you to open the Documentation in SAP GUI, Share a link etc.

Once all the details of the Domain are filled, you can Save and Activate the object. Once created, the object can also be viewed and changed in SE11.

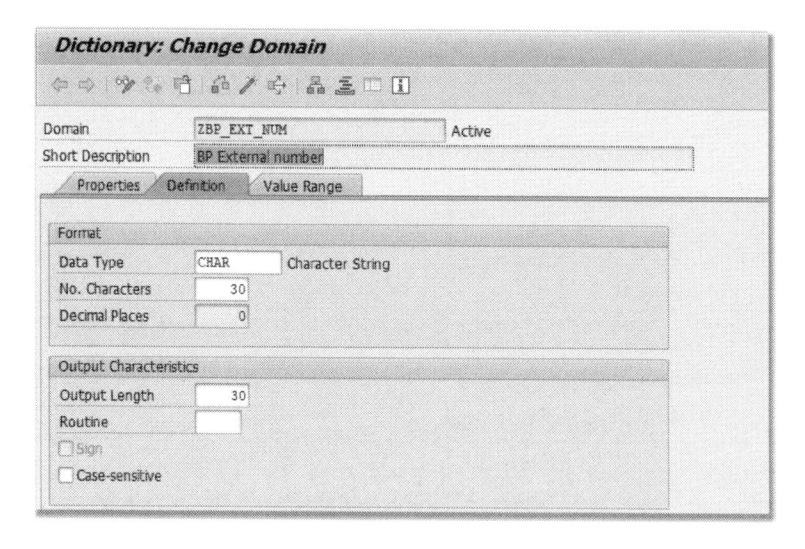

Figure 11: View Domain in SAP GUI

2.2 Creating Data Elements

The process for creating Data Elements is same as that for Domain. However, let us go through one more example.

This time, let us use the context menu on the 'Dictionary' folder created for the project.

Right click on the Dictionary folder and then click on New -> Data Element, as shown in Figure 12.

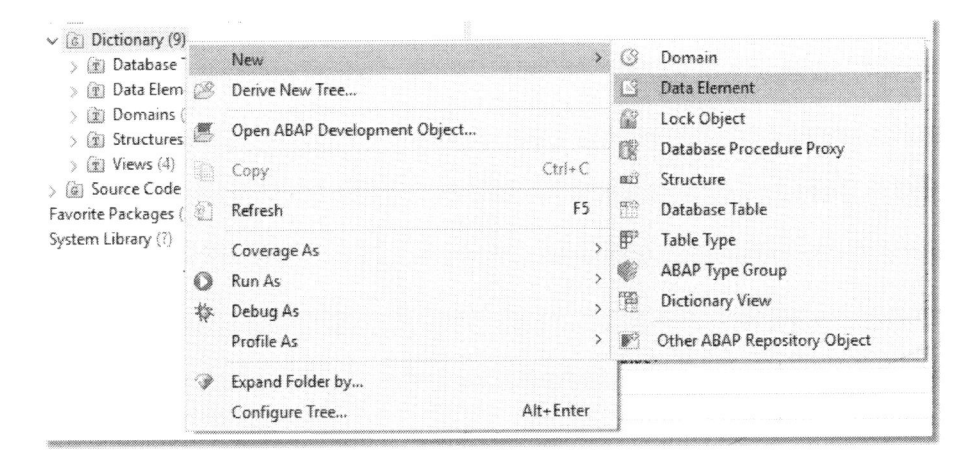

Figure 12: Create Data Element

As you see, this time all the DDIC artifacts are already listed and need not be searched. The system understands the context and provides the correct options.

Select 'Data Element' option. A new dialog box opens where you can specify the name and description of the Data Element.

Figure 13: Create Data Element

On clicking on Finish, a new Form opens where you could provide the details of the data element.

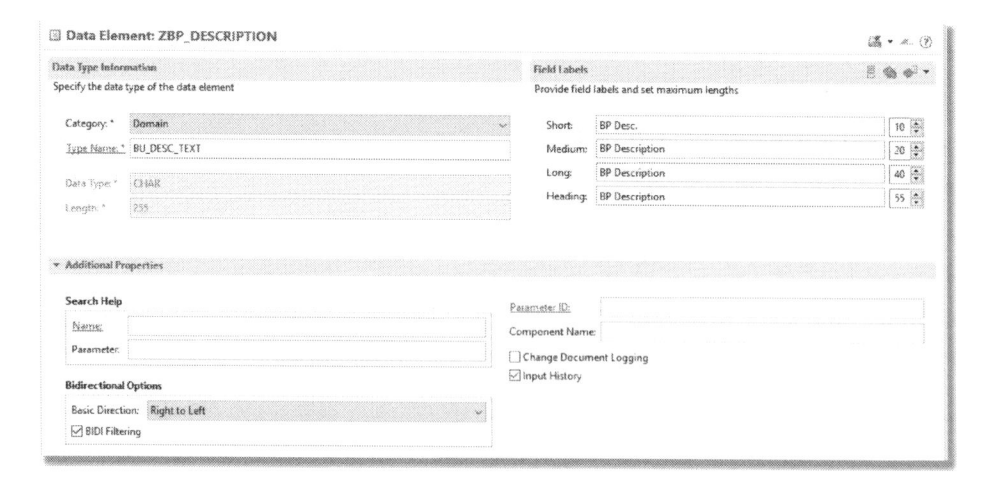

Figure 14: Enter Data Element details

Even for a first-time user, the UI is very intuitive and easy to use. In SE11, you must navigate between different tabs to fill the relevant information. In Eclipse all the necessary data can be filled in one screen and this eases the creation of the object.

Once the relevant details are filled, you could save and active the object (just like SE11).

2.3 Creating Structures

To Create a structure, right click on the dictionary folder and select Structure.

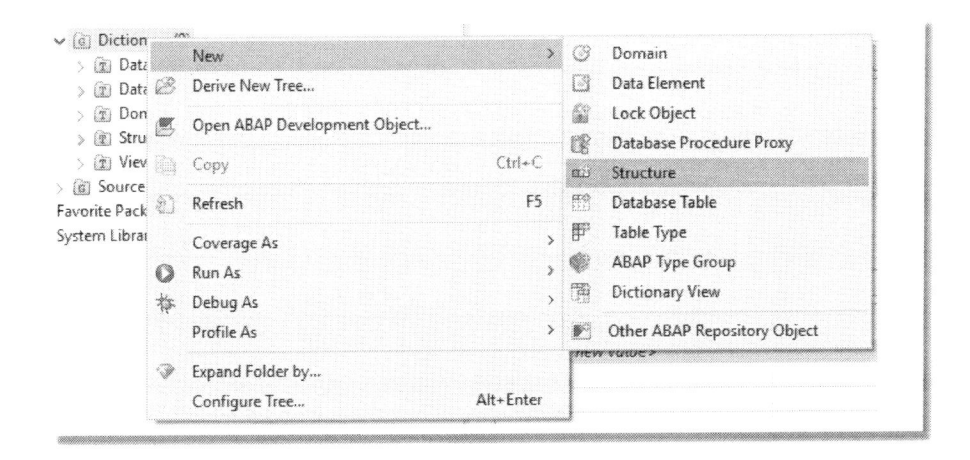

Figure 15: Create New Structure

Enter the name and Description of the structure and click on Finish (just like the other DDIC objects).

It is interesting to note that this time the user is not presented with a Form to fill out the structure components. Creating a DDIC structure in Eclipse is like creating a TYPE in ABAP.

The initial code looks like as below:

```
@EndUserText.label : 'Business Partner address'
@AbapCatalog.enhancementCategory : #NOT_EXTENSIBLE
define structure zbp_address {
  component_to_be_changed : abap.string(0);

}
```

During the creation, the provided short description is inserted and is displayed as an Annotation.

An Annotation is an instruction that is evaluated by frameworks. Annotations start with a @ and can be assigned to the whole structure or single components.

The second annotation is the Enhancement Category. By default, the Enhancement Category is selected as 'NOT_EXTENSIBLE. This can be changed, as required, by deleting the current enhancement category and selecting one of the options using the Code-Completion Feature. The options can are available when the user presses CTRL + Space.

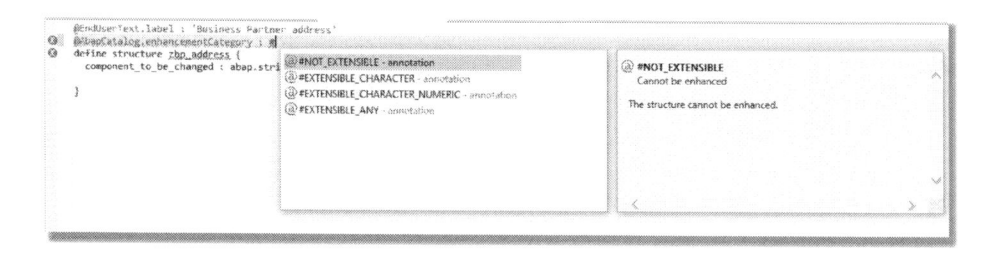

Figure 16: Enter Structure Enhancement Category

Now you can enter the different components of the structure in Curly brackets.

> @EndUserText.label : 'Business Partner address'
> @AbapCatalog.enhancementCategory : #NOT_EXTENSIBLE
> **define structure** zbp_address {
>   city1   : ad_city1;
>   city_code : ad_citynum;
>   post_code1 : ad_pstcd1;
>   po_box_num : ad_pobxnum;
>   street   : ad_street;
>   house_num1 : ad_hsnm1;
>   location : ad_lctn;
>   building : ad_bldng;
>   floor   : ad_floor;
>   roomnumber : ad_roomnum;
>   country   : land1;
>
> }

Save and activate the structure. The structure is now created and can be edited in SE11

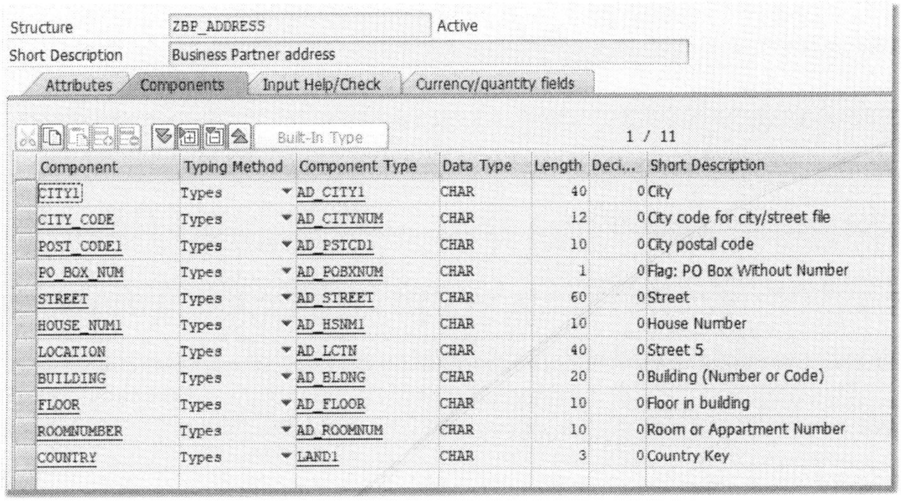

Structure	ZBP_ADDRESS		Active			
Short Description	Business Partner address					

Attributes | Components | Input Help/Check | Currency/quantity fields

1 / 11

Component	Typing Method	Component Type	Data Type	Length	Deci...	Short Description
CITY1	Types	AD_CITY1	CHAR	40	0	City
CITY_CODE	Types	AD_CITYNUM	CHAR	12	0	City code for city/street file
POST_CODE1	Types	AD_PSTCD1	CHAR	10	0	City postal code
PO_BOX_NUM	Types	AD_POBXNUM	CHAR	1	0	Flag: PO Box Without Number
STREET	Types	AD_STREET	CHAR	60	0	Street
HOUSE_NUM1	Types	AD_HSNM1	CHAR	10	0	House Number
LOCATION	Types	AD_LCTN	CHAR	40	0	Street 5
BUILDING	Types	AD_BLDNG	CHAR	20	0	Building (Number or Code)
FLOOR	Types	AD_FLOOR	CHAR	10	0	Floor in building
ROOMNUMBER	Types	AD_ROOMNUM	CHAR	10	0	Room or Appartment Number
COUNTRY	Types	LAND1	CHAR	3	0	Country Key

Figure 17: View Structure in SAP GUI

Right now, you might be wondering that the ABAP dictionary provides the options to provide 'Input Help/Check' and 'Currency/quantity fields'. Hence it should also be possible to add this in Eclipse. It wouldn't make sense to create the components in Eclipse and add other details via SAP GUI.

For our example, let us add an Input help for the field 'CITY_CODE'.

As you can see from Fig 2.18, the help for city code is not available in SE11.

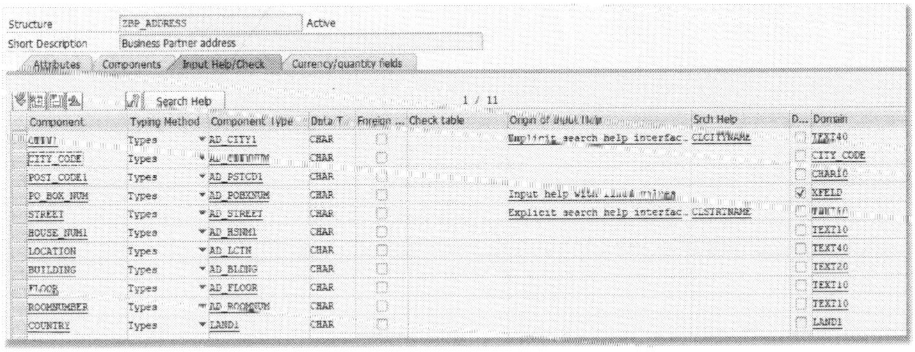

Figure 18: Input Help of Structure

The Input help can be added by using the suffixes "with value help" or "with foreign key" after the component type.

The various attributes which are added in the Form based approach in SE11 can also be added here. E.g. we can add that the check is a non-key check and is applicate only to screens by using annotations.

The final code is as shown below:

```
@EndUserText.label : 'Business Partner address'
@AbapCatalog.enhancementCategory : #NOT_EXTENSIBLE
define structure zbp_address {
  city1     : ad_city1;
  @AbapCatalog.foreignKey.keyType : #NON_KEY
  @AbapCatalog.foreignKey.screenCheck : true
  city_code : ad_citynum
    with foreign key [0..*,0..1] adrcity
      where country = zbp_address.country
        and city_code = zbp_address.city_code;
  post_code1 : ad_pstcd1;
  po_box_num : ad_pobxnum;
  street     : ad_street;
  house_num1 : ad_hsnm1;
  location   : ad_lctn;
  building   : ad_bldng;
  floor      : ad_floor;
  roomnumber : ad_roomnum;
  country    : land1;

}
```

Now Save and Activate the structure.

The DDIC structure is changed and the changes can be viewed in SE11.

Figure 19: View New Input help in SAP GUI

2.4 Creating Classes

To create an ABAP class, use the menu option File -> New -> ABAP Class

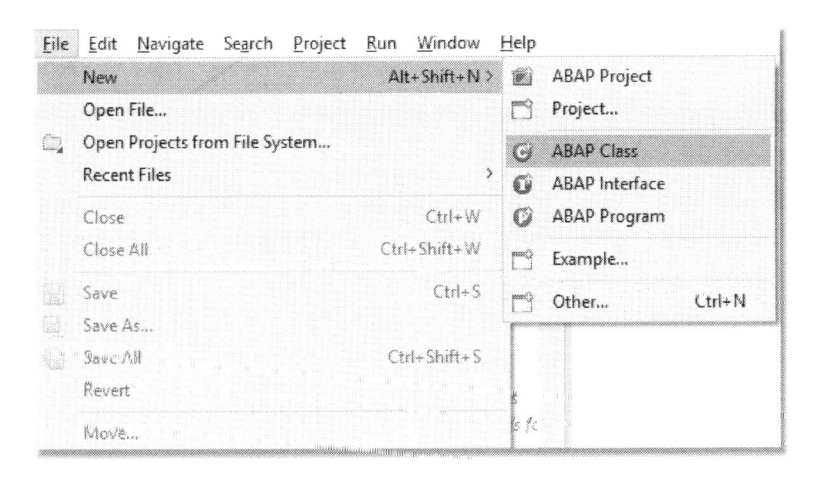

Figure 20: Create New ABAP Class

Enter the name and description of the class and click on Finish.

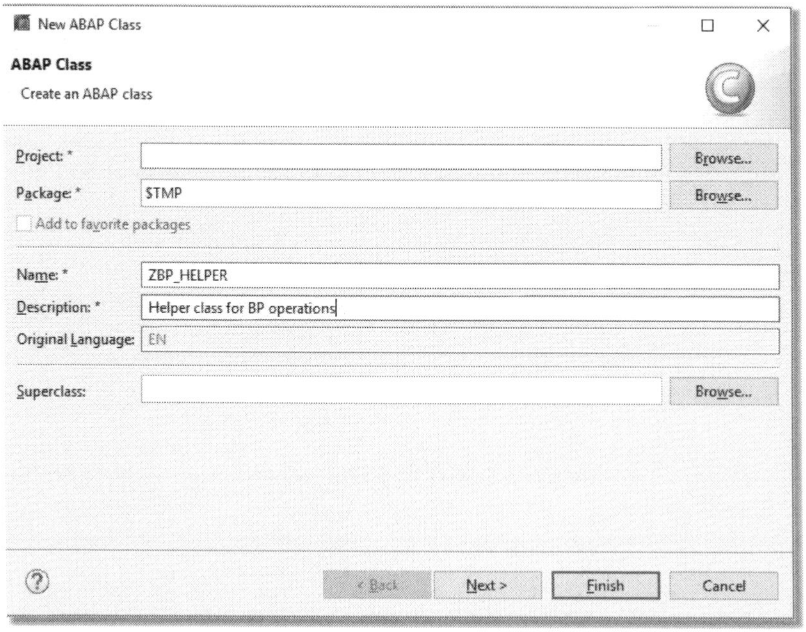

Figure 21: Enter details of new Class

Here, you would notice that the generated code has blocks for both Definition and Implementation. In SE24, the definition was Form-based, but here the definition and implementation of the class is a big block of code (something like an ABAP program).

Although it might seem complex for the old time ABAP programmers, it is quite simple once you get used to it.

```
CLASS zbp_helper DEFINITION
  PUBLIC
  FINAL
  CREATE PUBLIC .

  PUBLIC SECTION.
  PROTECTED SECTION.
  PRIVATE SECTION.
ENDCLASS.


CLASS zbp_helper IMPLEMENTATION.
```

ENDCLASS.

Let us add a method to add a Role to the BP. In SE24, you would have added the Method in the list of methods in the class and then proceeded to write the code in the method. Here as well, the steps are same, but it is code based.

Let us create a public method 'ADD_BP_ROLE'. This method would take the BP number and Role as an input and return a Success or Failure Flag.

The code in the class definition would be as shown in Fig 2.22:

```
▶ ZBP_HELPER ▶
CLASS zbp_helper DEFINITION
    PUBLIC
    FINAL
    CREATE PUBLIC .

    PUBLIC SECTION.
      METHODS add_bp_role
        IMPORTING bp_id   TYPE bu_partner
                  bp_role TYPE bu_partnerrole
        EXPORTING message TYPE char1         .

    PROTECTED SECTION.
    PRIVATE SECTION.
ENDCLASS.


CLASS zbp_helper IMPLEMENTATION.
ENDCLASS.
```

Figure 22: View Class Definition

Note that although the definition is complete, there is no implementation. The editor also shows an error. You could either create an implementation yourself or let the editor help you.

In this example, we use the Editor code completion feature to create the implementation.

Click on the Icon beside the method and chose the option 'Add implementation ….'.

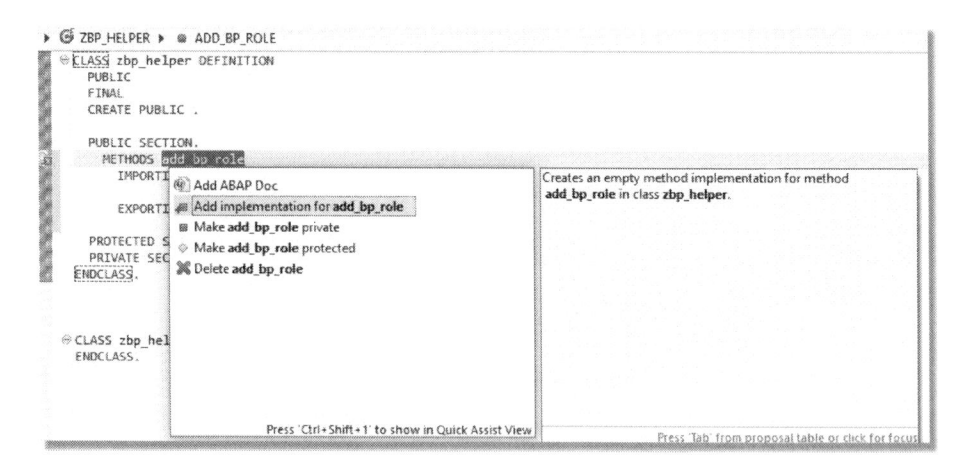

Figure 23: Add Implementation

This creates the method implementation. Now you can add Save and activate the class.

Once successfully activated, we can Display / Edit the class in SAP GUI as well.

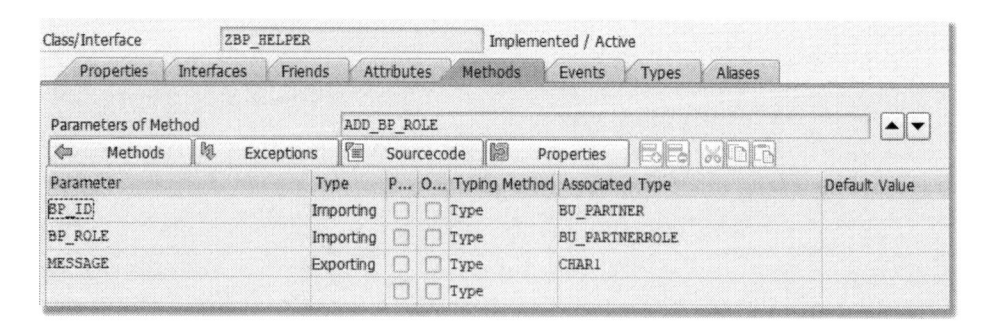

Figure 24: View Class in SAP GUI

2.5 Deleting Unused Variables

Maintaining the quality of the code is very important to ensure its functional correctness and maintainability. Hence before a code can be delivered, it is important to clean up the code.

If you run an ATC or Extended checks, you can find the errors and warnings in your program. One such check which keeps popping up is the 'Deletion of Unused variables'. In extended check, this comes as a Warning and requires us to navigate back and forth to delete the unwanted variables. If the code is big, then the context of the code is lost, and we might have to run the Extended check again. This activity consumes a lot of time and can be done very quickly in Eclipse.

To Delete the unused Variables, we can now use the menu path Source Code -> Delete Unused variables.

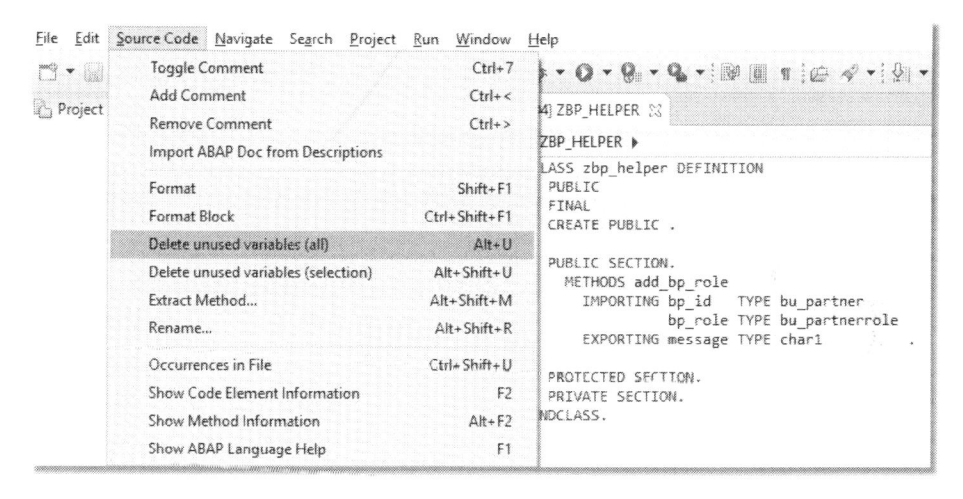

Figure 25: Delete Unused Variables

2.6 Searching for Objects

Often you need to search for objects (Standard SAP delivered object or Custom object). In SAP GUI you can simply go to the related transaction and search for it. E.g. If I wanted to search for a Function module then I could go to Transaction SE37 and search for the appropriate FM. In Eclipse editor, we do not have such specific transactions. But it is possible to search for objects using the menu option Navigate -> Open ABAP Development Object.

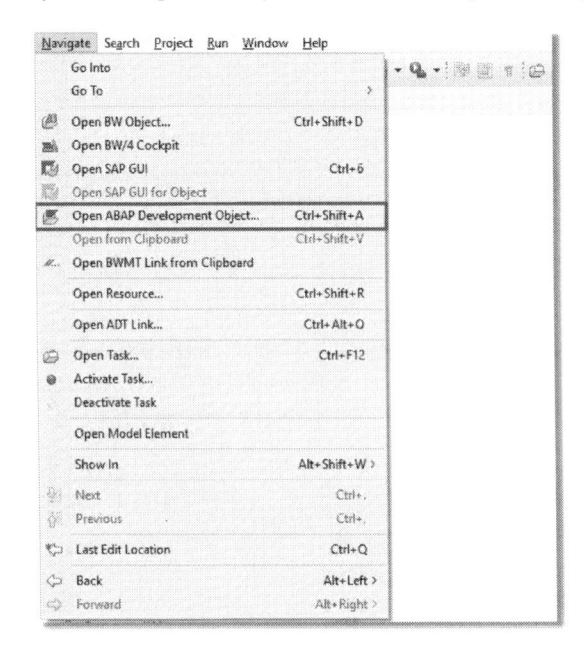

Figure 26: Search ABAP Development Objects

This opens a dialog, where you could enter the search string to find the object.

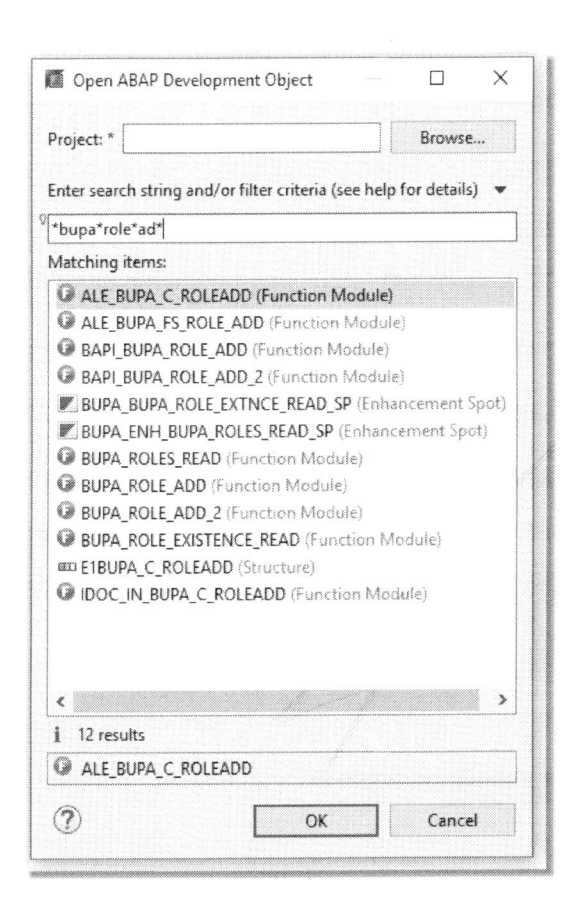

Figure 27: Open ABAP Development Object

2.7 Formatting ABAP Source Code

In Eclipse the 'Pretty Printer' is called 'Source Formatter'.

You can do the formatting from the editor of a development object in the following ways:

1. To format the whole ABAP source code, use the Source Code -> Format menu.

2. To format selected source code blocks, select them and use the Source Code -> Format Block menu.

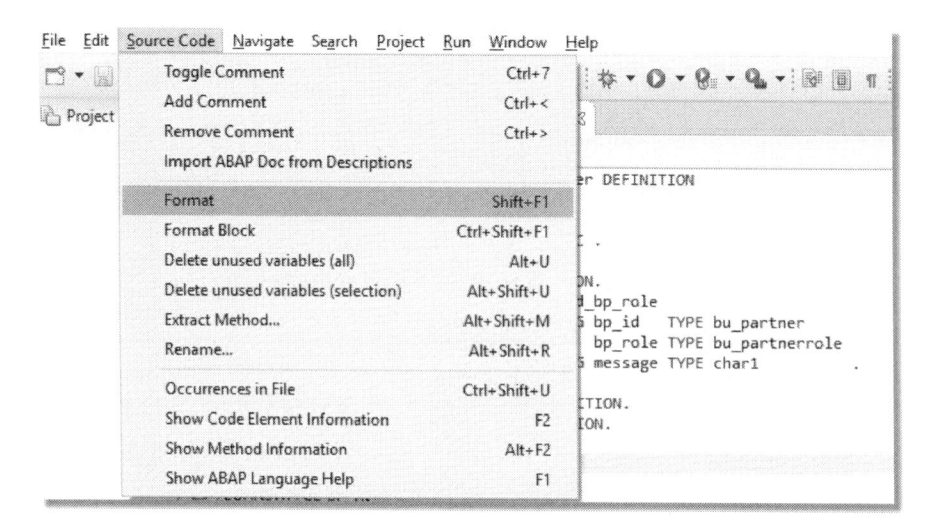

Figure 28: Formatting ABAP Source Code

2.8 Using Where-used List

You can get the Where-used list either by using the context menu or by using the button on the Applicate toolbar.

Figure 2.29 shows the context menu option:

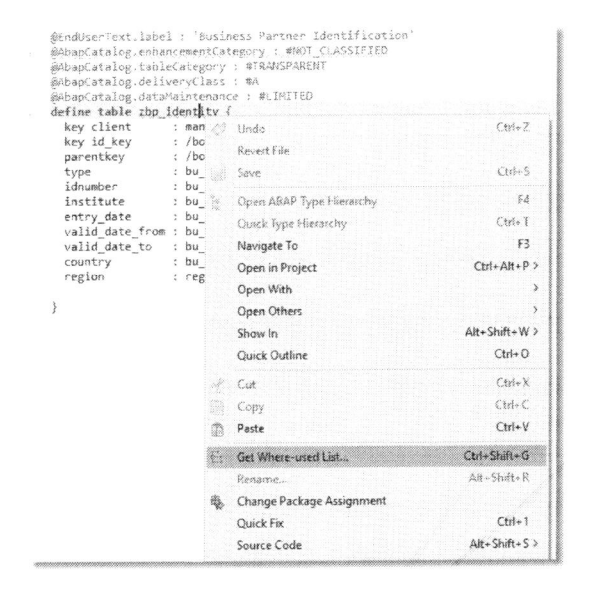

Figure 29: Where-used List

The Where used list is then displayed as shown in Fig 2.30. It is also possible to navigate to the objects from the where-used list.

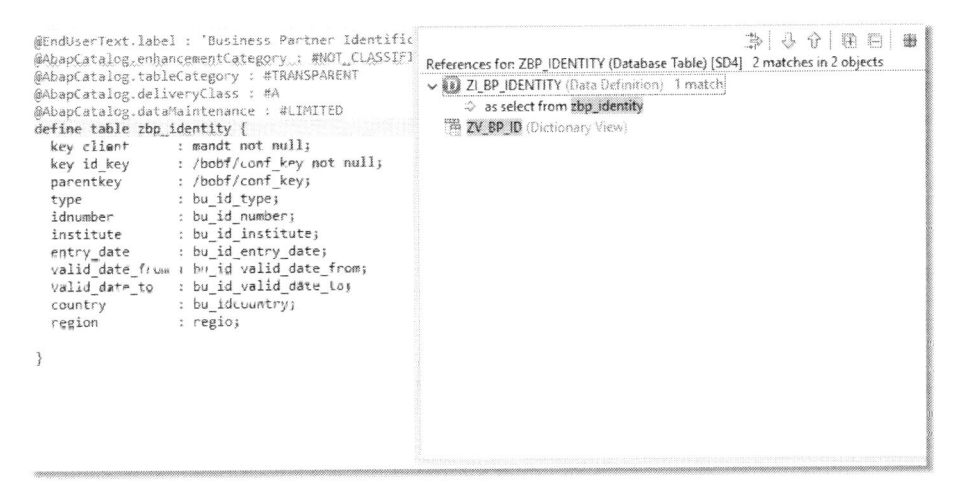

Figure 30: Where-used list results

2.9 Navigating to SAP GUI

It is possible to navigate from Eclipse to SAP GUI with the buttons on the menu bar.

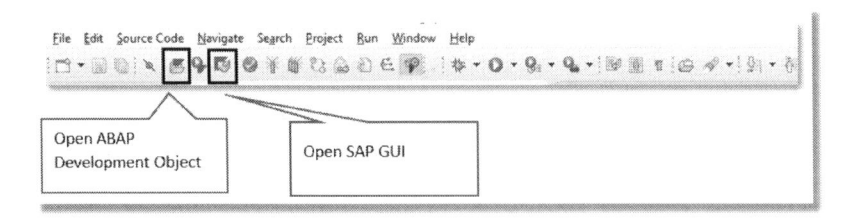

Figure 31: Navigate to SAP GUI

- The Open ABAP development object option allows you to search and display the object directly.

    e.g. If we want to navigate to transaction SE37, then we can type that in the search string and click on OK.

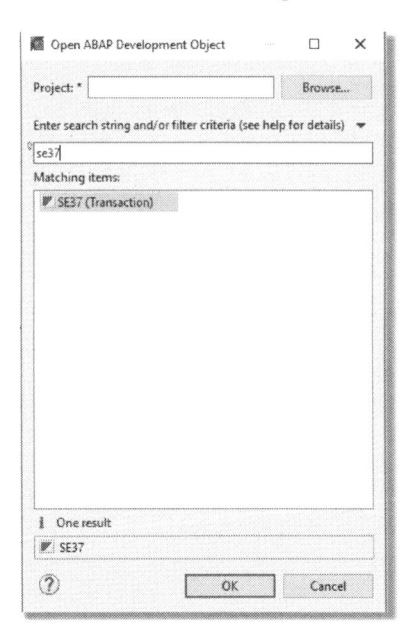

Figure 32: Open ABAP Development Object

The system then open SAP GUI in Eclipse.

- The Open SAP GUI option just opens the SAP GUI. You can then navigate the relevant SAP transaction by entering the transaction.

3. Summary

In this chapter we covered the Installation process and Basics of using Eclipse for ABAP. This chapter is just an introduction to using Eclipse and should form a basis for further exploration by the ABAP developers.

It is very clear that SAP wants Eclipse to be 'The Development Environment' for ABAP. Hence, it becomes very important that SAP Developers get used to using Eclipse.

Chapter 2: New ABAP 7.4 and 7.5 Language Features

With the release of ABAP 7.4 and 7.5 several new ABAP language features have been introduced. These new language statements improve the existing ABAP syntax and adds new language capabilities.

These are easy to use and reduces the number of lines we need to code to achieve the same functionality. The new language features have been added without taking away the old syntax (ensuring backward compatibility).

1. New Language Features

1.1 Inline Declarations

It had always been considered as a practice in SAP to declare the variables at the beginning of the program. But most developers ended up declaring the variables, just before using it. With inline declarations SAP has made this practice acceptable and the preferred way of declaration.

Inline declarations are a new way of declaring variables and field symbols. This enables the programmers to declare the variable at the time when they are required, as opposed to declaring it at the start of the program.

The data type of most of the variables are knows as they are either changing parameters of a procedure or the values are assigned from an existing variable. Hence, the compiler knows what to check against. Thus, with the new language statements it makes sense to let the compiler derive the type of the new variables without having to declare it explicitly.

Let us look at the below example where we want to assign a value to the variable:

Example 1: Assign value to a variable

    Before release 7.40

```
DATA l_str_val TYPE string.
l_str_val = 'Hello World'.
```

With release 7.40

    DATA(l_str_val) = 'Hello World'.

With the above new feature, the complier already knows that it can and needs to store the value of 'Hello World' in a String variable. Hence, there is no explicit need to declare a variable of type String.

The above code does not only reduce the number of lines but is also easier to understand.

Let us look at another example where we have to loop over an internal table and assign a value to the work area.

Example 2: Loop over an internal table

    Before release 7.40

```
DATA l_wa LIKE LINE OF i_tab.
LOOP AT i_tab INTO l_wa.
  ...
ENDLOOP.
```

    With release 7.40

```
LOOP AT i_tab INTO DATA (l_wa).
  ...
ENDLOOP.
```

Every time we need to loop over an internal table we need to declare a work area. Many a times this work area is also not of any use once the loop processing is complete.

Hence with inline declarations it makes it easy to declare it and use when it is required.

Below are some more examples of inline declarations:

Example 3: Loop over internal table and assign it to a field symbol

    Before release 7.40

FIELD-SYMBOLS: <f_line> TYPE ....

LOOP AT i_tab ASSIGNING <f_line>.
...
ENDLOOP.

With release 7.40

LOOP AT i_tab ASSIGNING FIELD-SYMBOL(<f_line>).
...
ENDLOOP.

This is similar to Example 2, except that it uses Field symbols instead of work area.

Example 4: Read a line of internal table and assign it to a field symbol

Before release 7.40

FIELD-SYMBOLS: <line> TYPE ....

READ TABLE i_tab ASSIGNING <line>.

With release 7.40

READ TABLE i_tab ASSIGNING FIELD-SYMBOL(<line>).

Example 5: Select from database into an internal table

Before release 7.40

DATA: i_tab TYPE TABLE OF dtab.

SELECT * FROM dtab
  INTO TABLE i_tab
  WHERE fld = lv_fld.

With release 7.40

SELECT * FROM dtab
  INTO TABLE @DATA(i_tab)
  WHERE fld = @lv_fld.

You would have noticed that you would have to put @ symbol in front of your variables (or constants) used in select statements when using the new features. This helps the complier in understanding that we are not referring to the fields in the database but variables in the program.

Example 5: Select specific fields from database into an internal table

    Before release 7.40

```
SELECT SINGLE field1 field2
  FROM dbtab
  INTO  (lv_field1 , lv_field2)
  WHERE ...

WRITE: / lv_field1, lv_field2.
```

    With release 7.40

```
SELECT SINGLE field1 AS fld1,
       field2 AS fld2
  FROM dbtab
  INTO @DATA(ls_structure)
  WHERE …

WRITE: / ls_structure-fld1, ls_structure-fld2
```

Please note that when using new features, you also must put commas between the fields you are retrieving from the database and put the INTO statement at the end.

1.2 Internal Tables

In previous section we saw that it was possible to read the internal table into a work area without having to declare the work area before the read statement. This change would remove extra data declaration lines.

However, if you adopt the new features completely, you might never have to use the read statement.

Below are some examples:

Example 1: Reading a row from an internal table using index

Before release 7.40

    READ TABLE i_tab INDEX idx
    INTO wa.

With release 7.40

    wa = i_tab[idx].

Example 2: Assign value to a variable

Before release 7.40

    READ TABLE i_tab INDEX idx
    USING KEY key
    INTO wa.

With release 7.40

    wa = i_tab[KEY key INDEX idx].

Example 3: Reading a table with key

Before release 7.40

    READ TABLE i_tab
    WITH KEY col1 = ...
    col2 = ...
    INTO wa.

With release 7.40

    wa = i_tab[col1 = ... col2 = ...].

Example 4: Check if a line exists

Before release 7.40

    READ TABLE i_tab ...
    TRANSPORTING NO FIELDS.

```
IF sy-subrc = 0.
  ...
ENDIF.
```

With release 7.40

```
IF line_exists( i_tab[ ... ] ).
  ...
ENDIF.
```

Example 5: Get table index

Before release 7.40

```
DATA i_dx type sy-tabix.
READ TABLE ...
  TRANSPORTING NO FIELDS.
I_dx = sy-tabix.
```

With release 7.40

```
DATA(i_dx) =
  line_index( i_tab[ ... ] ).
```

The above new language features come with a catch that if the value is not found then an exception (CX_SY_ITAB_LINE_NOT_FOUND) is raised and if the exception is not caught then there will be a short dump.

Therefore, SAP recommends that the value should be assigned to a field symbol and then we could check the value using sy-subrc.

```
ASSIGN I_tab[ 1 ] to FIELD-SYMBOL(<ls_tab>).
IF sy-subrc = 0.

ENDIF.
```

1.3 String Processing

String processing is very frequently used in ABAP code. The data from the database often needs to be formatted before it is displayed to the user and vice versa. E.g. if we have to display the sales order details on the screen, then we might have to concatenate a text with the Sales order number and then display it.

Following are some instances where string processing are required:

- Convert Input data before using it in Database operations

- Convert data from data base into a more human readable form.

1.3.1 Concatenation of strings

Concatenation is simplified in ABAP 7.4. In some cases, they replace the old way of concatenating and in other cases they also introduce new functionality.

Below are some important changes:

- String Templates: the option to create a character string out of literal texts, expressions, and control characters.

- Chaining Operator: chain two character-like operands into one new character string.

- Character String Functions: built-in functions for searching, processing and comparing strings.

CONCATENATE prior to ABAP 7.4

One of the common uses of concatenate statement is to display the data in a more human readable form.
Let us take an example where you need to show the Sales order number to the user. Just displaying the order number in the screen might not be the best. Hence, you might be required to concatenate some literals.

```
DATA: lv_order TYPE string,
      lv_out   TYPE string.

lv_order = l_vbak-vbeln.


CONCATENATE 'Your Sales order number is:'
        lv_order
        INTO lv_out
```

SEPARATED BY space.

WRITE:/ lv_out.

```
Your Sales order number is: 0000005723
```

CONCATENATE ABAP 7.4

DATA: lv_order TYPE string,
  lv_out   TYPE string.

lv_order = l_vbak-vbeln.

lv_out = |Your Sales order number is:| && lv_order.

WRITE:/ lv_out.

```
Your Sales order number is: 0000005723
```

As you would have noticed, ABAP now has a new concatenation operator, &&.

String Templates

The purpose of a string template is to create a new character string out of literal texts and embedded expressions. It largely replaces the use of the WRITE TO statement.

A string template is defined by using the | (pipe) symbol at the beginning and end of a template.

DATA: character_string TYPE string.
character_string = |This is a literal text.|.

This example has in fact the same result as:

character_string = `This is a literal text.`.

The added value of a string template becomes clear when combining literal texts with embedded expressions and control characters. Embedded expressions are defined within a string template with curly brackets *{ expression }*. Note that a space between bracket and expression is obligatory.

An expression can be a data object (variable), a functional method, a predefined function or a calculation expression. Some examples are:

character_string = |{ a_numeric_variable }|.

character_string = |This resulted in return code { sy–subrc }|.

character_string = |The length of text element 001 ({ text–001 }) is { strlen(text–001) }|.

Embedded expressions have a default output format, but also several formatting options, comparable to the format options of the WRITE statement.

Example:

DATA: comm_capital   TYPE bzusage VALUE '1234567.123',
      currency_field TYPE swhr,
      lv_string   TYPE string.

lv_string = |{ comm_capital CURRENCY = currency_field NUMBER = USER }|.

The above code snippet converts the amount in a display format as per user settings.

The value of the amount is assigned in the declaration as '1234567.123'.

This is converted into '1.234.567,12' after the String operation.

Chaining Operator

The Chaining Operator && can be used to create one-character string out of multiple other strings and string templates.

In this example, a number text, a space, an existing character string and a new string template are concatenated into a new character string.

character_string = 'Text literal'(002) && ` ` && character_string && |{ amount_field NUMBER = USER }|.

1.3.2 ALPHA Formatting

Formatting functions CONVERSION_EXIT_ALPHA_INPUT and CONVERSION_EXIT_ALPHA_OUTPUT is used very frequently to add and remove leading zeroes from data. It adds to the number of lines of code but does not provide much business logic. E.g. it might be required to remove the zeroes when showing messages to the user, but then add them back before you read the database.

Remove leading zeroes before output to user

```
l_ordernum = '0000012345'.

CALL FUNCTION 'CONVERSION_EXIT_ALPHA_OUTPUT'
  EXPORTING
    input    = l_ordernum
  IMPORTING
    OUTPUT   = l_ordernum.
```

Add leading zeroes back before database read

```
l_ordernum = '12345'.

CALL FUNCTION 'CONVERSION_EXIT_ALPHA_INPUT'
  EXPORTING
    input    = l_ordernum
  IMPORTING
    OUTPUT   = l_ordernum.
```

The above can be done in a much simpler manner.

Remove Leading zeros

```
DATA(lv_vbeln) = '0000012345'.
lv_vbeln = / |{ lv_vbeln ALPHA = OUT }|.
```

Add leading zeros

```
DATA(lv_vbeln) = '12345'.
lv_vbeln = |{ lv_vbeln ALPHA = IN }|.
```

1.4 Calling functions

1.4.1 Method chaining

During the processing of a Class method or a Function module you will need to execute more granular Function modules, Class methods, form routines etc.

Many a times, the values returned from one call needs to be passed as an input to the next call. Hence the developer ends up creating temporary variables. These variables do not add any value but are just used in receiving data from one call and passing it to the next call.

With ABAP 7.02, SAP introduced Method chaining. With this, the user could pass the values without the use of temporary variables.

Let us look at the below example of old way of coding.

e.g. we need to get the email id of the business partner and then pass it to the email service. This would require getting the email and store it in the local variable. Then this value would be passed to the email method.

```
l_bp_emailid = lo_bp->get_email( i_bp = l_bp ).
lo_email->send_email( l_bp_emailid ).
```

With Method chaining you can achieve the same results as follows:

```
lo_email->send_email( lo_bp->get_email( i_bp = l_bp ) ).
```

1.4.2 Avoiding type mismatch dumps when calling functions

ABAPers are familiar with the Type Mismatch dump which happens if the type of the variable does not match with the parameter definition of the Function Modules. With a method, you get a syntax error; with a function module, you get a short dump at runtime. The process of checking the data types of the parameters, declaring the variables and resolving these dumps are quite tedious and not required.

Since the compiler already knows which types are expected, it would be best to allow the compiler to decide the data type.

e.g.

```
CALL METHOD lo_bus_partner->update_address(
  EXPORTING
    i_address  = wa_address
  IMPORTING
    e_message  = DATA(lo_message)
       ).
```

As you can see from the above example the variable for the message was not declared with a DATA statement.

1.5 CONVersion Operator

Conversion operator converts a value into a specified type. It is suitable for avoiding the declaration of helper variables.

For Example, let us assume that a method expects a string, but you have the data in a text field. As per the old syntax you would need to move the value to a string variable and then pass this helper variable to the method call. With CONV operator the helper variable is no more required.

<u>Before release 7.40</u>

```
DATA cust_name TYPE c LENGTH 20.
DATA helper TYPE string.

helper = cust_name.

cl_func=>process_func( i_name = helper ).
```

In the above code snippet, cust_name is a character of length 20. But the method process_function expects a string. Hence in the old syntax it was required to move the data to a variable which was type compatible with the method parameters.

With release 7.40

> DATA cust_name TYPE c LENGTH 20.
>
> cl_func=>process_func(i_name = CONV string(cust_name)).
>
> In such cases it is even simpler to write
>
> DATA cust_name TYPE c LENGTH 20.
>
> cl_func=>process_func(i_name = CONV #(cust_name)).

With the new syntax, the helper variable (helper) is not required. The value can be converted directly during the method call.

The syntax of the CONV operator is as follows:

… CONV dtype|#(…) …

If the value of the type can be derived (as in our example) then the data type ('dtype') is not required. It is sufficient to use the '#'.

1.6 CASTing Operator

The casting operator CAST is a constructor operator that performs a down cast or an up cast for the argument object and creates a reference variable as a result.

The syntax of the CASTing operator is as follows:

… CAST #/type(/let exp/ dobj) …

The 'type' can be specified as:

- Class or an Interface.
- The '#' character is a symbol for the operand 'type'. This can be used only when the operand type is unique and fully identifiable.
- any non-generic data type dtype or the fully generic data type data

Example of Down Cast

Let us assume that you need all the components of a structure. This is done by getting the metadata of the structure by calling method CL_ABAP_STRUCTDESCR=> DESCRIBE_BY_NAME. This returns a reference to description object TYPE REF TO CL_ABAP_TYPEDESCR. The returned reference can be used to get the components of the structure.

Before release 7.40

>
> DATA structdescr TYPE REF TO cl_abap_structdescr.
>
> structdescr ?= cl_abap_typedescr=>describe_by_name('ZBP_STRUCT').
>
> DATA components TYPE abap_compdescr_tab.
>
> components = structdescr->components.

In the above code we first get the details of the structure in a helper variable structdescr and then use this to get the components.

With release 7.40

>
> DATA(components) = CAST cl_abap_structdescr(cl_abap_typedescr=>describe_by_name('ZBP_STRUCT'))->components.

With the new syntax you do not need the helper variable structdescr.

1.7 VALUE Operator

The value operator VALUE is a constructor operator that creates a value for the type specified with 'type'.

You could construct an initial value for any data type.

Example 1: Create an internal table and fill it with initial values as shown below:

TYPES char_tab TYPE TABLE OF char20 WITH EMPTY KEY.

DATA(chardata) = VALUE char_tab(('Firstrow') ('Secondrow') ('Thirdrow')).

Table	CHARDATA
Attributes	Standard [3x1(40)]

Row	TABLE_LINE [C(20)]
1	Firstrow
2	Secondrow
3	Thirdrow

Example 2: Create an internal table, where for each line a value can be assigned.

TYPES: BEGIN OF t_struct,
       col1 TYPE char10,
       col2 TYPE char10,
    END OF t_struct.

DATA itab TYPE TABLE OF t_struct.

itab = VALUE #((col1 = 'Col1Row1' col2 = 'Col2Row1')
                (col1 = 'Col1Row2' col2 = 'Col2Row2')).

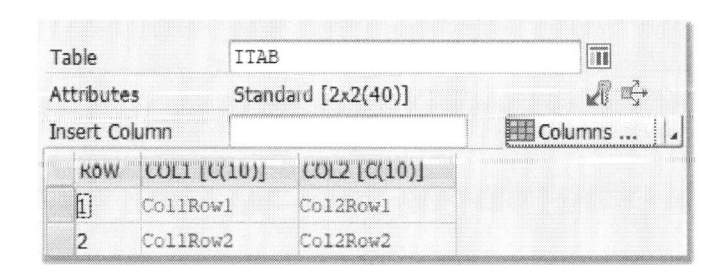

Table	ITAB
Attributes	Standard [2x2(40)]

Row	COL1 [C(10)]	COL2 [C(10)]
1	Col1Row1	Col2Row1
2	Col1Row2	Col2Row2

Example 3: Construct a ranges table and fills it with four rows while using the short form for structured row types.

```
DATA itab TYPE RANGE OF i.

itab = VALUE #( sign = 'I'  option = 'BT' ( low = 1  high = 10 )
                            ( low = 21 high = 30 )
                            ( low = 41 high = 50 )
                 option = 'GE' ( low = 61 ) ).
```

Row	SIGN [C(1)]	OPTION [C(2)]	LOW [I(4)]	HIGH [I(4)]
1	I	BT	1	10
2	I	BT	21	30
3	I	BT	41	50
4	I	GE	61	0

Note that you cannot construct elementary values (which is possible with instantiation operator NEW) – simply because there is no need for it.

1.8 FOR operator

FOR operator is used to loop at an internal table. For each loop the row is read and assigned to a Work area or a field symbol. This is similar to the FOR loop we would have used in C language.

Example 1: Transfer our data from one internal table to another

Before 7.4 we had to loop over the first table, assign the value to the work area of the new table and then append the work area into the new table.
e.g.

```
LOOP AT lt_sales ASSIGNING FIELD-SYMBOL(<fs_sales>).
```

```
            lv_sales_no = <fs_sales>-vbeln.

            APPEND lv_sales_no TO lt_all_sales.

            CLEAR : lv_sales_no.

        ENDLOOP.
```

In the new syntax the above operation can be done as shown below:

```
        DATA(lt_all_sales) = VALUE tt_sales( FOR ls_sales IN lt_sales ( ls_sales-vbeln )
        ).
```


Example 2: For with Where condition

```
TYPES:
  BEGIN OF ty_business_partner,
    partner TYPE char10,
    name    TYPE char30,
    city    TYPE char30,
    route   TYPE char10,
  END   OF ty_business_partner.

TYPES: tt_bus_partner TYPE SORTED TABLE OF ty_business_partner
        WITH UNIQUE KEY partner.

TYPES: tt_citys TYPE STANDARD TABLE OF char30 WITH EMPTY KEY.

DATA(t_BP) =
  VALUE tt_bus_partner(
    ( partner = 'BP0001' name = 'PeterParker' city = 'NY' route = 'R0001' )
    ( partner = 'BP0002' name = 'Superman'    city = 'LA'  route = 'R0003' )
    ( partner = 'BP0003' name = 'Batman'      city = 'DFW' route = 'R0001' )
    ( partner = 'BP0004' name = 'IronMan'     city = 'CH'  route = 'R0003' )
  ).

* FOR to get the column CITY
DATA(t_city) =
  VALUE tt_citys( FOR ls_bp IN t_BP WHERE ( route = 'R0001' ) ( ls_bp-city ) ).
```

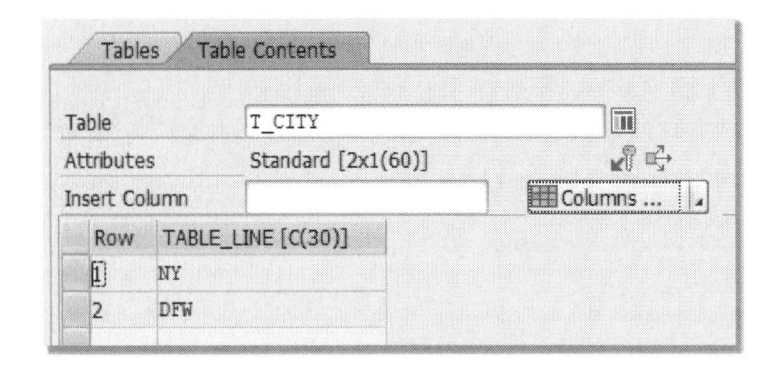

Tables	Table Contents		
Table	T_CITY		
Attributes	Standard [2x1(60)]		
Insert Column		Columns ...	
Row	TABLE_LINE [C(30)]		
1	NY		
2	DFW		

1.9 Reduction operator REDUCE

Reduce operator creates a result of specified data type after going through iterations. In classical ABAP if we had to evaluate the data in an internal table then we had to loop through the internal table, evaluate the condition and then take appropriate action. This could be done in a much simpler way with Reduce.

Syntax:

```
... REDUCE type(
INIT result = start_value
    ...
FOR for_exp1
FOR for_exp2
...
NEXT ...
    result = iterated_value
... )
```

Example 1: Count lines of table that meet a condition (field city contains "LA").

```
TYPES:
 BEGIN OF ty_business_partner,
   partner  TYPE char10,
   name     TYPE char30,
   city     TYPE char30,
   route    TYPE char10,
 END   OF ty_business_partner.
```

```
TYPES: tt_bus_partner TYPE SORTED TABLE OF ty_business_partner
       WITH UNIQUE KEY partner.

DATA(t_BP) =
 VALUE tt_bus_partner(
   ( partner = 'BP0001' name = 'PeterParker' city = 'NY'  route = 'R0001' )
   ( partner = 'BP0002' name = 'Superman'    city = 'LA'  route = 'R0003' )
   ( partner = 'BP0003' name = 'Batman'      city = 'DFW' route = 'R0001' )
   ( partner = 'BP0004' name = 'IronMan'     city = 'LA'  route = 'R0003' )
 ).

" Before 7.40
DATA: lv_lines TYPE i.
LOOP AT t_bp INTO DATA(ls_bp) WHERE city = 'LA'.
  lv_lines = lv_lines + 1.
ENDLOOP.
```

With the new syntax it is not required to loop through all the records to count the number of matches.

The REDUCE operator can be used instead

```
DATA(lv_lines) = REDUCE i( INIT x = 0 FOR wa_bp IN t_BP
           WHERE ( city = 'LA' ) NEXT x = x + 1 ).
```

1.10 Conditional operators COND

It is an accepted practice in ABAP to use CASE statements instead of IF statement. CASE statements made the code readable but had an issue that it was not able to evaluate multiple conditions.

Hence in many instances, the ABAPers had to move back to using IF..ELSE..ENDIF constructs. Let us look at the below example:

```
DATA: lv_text(30).

IF lv_prod_catg = '10' AND lv_prodtype = 'A'.
   lv_text = 'Television'.
ELSE.
IF lv_prod_catg ='20' AND lv_prodtype = 'B'.
```

```
        lv_text = 'Automatic Washing Machine'
    ELSE.
    IF lv_prod_catg ='20' AND lv_prodtype = 'C'.
        lv_text = 'Semi-Automatic Washing Machine'.
          ..
        ENDIF.
```

The above conditions are not possible by using Case statements as the WHEN clause could only evaluate either the lv_prod_catg or the lv_prodtype. This is where the new COND operator comes handy. COND allows us to evaluate multiple variables.

Syntax:

```
    ... COND dtype|#( WHEN log_exp1 THEN result1
            [ WHEN log_exp2 THEN result2 ]
              ...
            [ ELSE resultn ] ) ...
```

Example 1:

```
TRY.

  DATA(lv_text) =
        COND #( WHEN lv_prod_catg = '10' AND lv_prodtype = 'A'
            THEN 'Television'
          WHEN lv_prod_catg ='20' AND lv_prodtype = 'B'
            THEN 'Automatic Washing Machine'
          WHEN lv_prod_catg ='20' AND lv_prodtype = 'C'
            THEN 'Semi-Automatic Washing Machine'
          ELSE THROW  cx_exception( ) ).
```

CATCH cx_exception.

ENDTRY.

1.11 Conditional operators SWITCH

SWITCH is a conditional operator like CASE but more powerful and with much less coding.

It is used to switch from one value to another, based on a condition.

Syntax:

> ... SWITCH dtype|#(operand
>   WHEN const1 THEN result1
>   [WHEN const2 THEN result2]
>   ...
>   [ELSE resultn]) ...

Example 1:

> DATA(lv_status) = SWITCH #(lv_flag
>   WHEN 'X' THEN 'Completed'
>   ELSE 'In Process'
>   ).

In the above example based on the value of the flag the value of the status is assigned to the lb_status variable.

1.12 Corresponding Operator

This operator allows the copy of data from one internal table to another internal table (just like move-corresponding) but provides more options on which columns are copied. With this new statement it is possible to not copy the values of one column even it the same column exists in the target internal table. It is also possible to copy data between columns which have different names in the source and target internal tables.

Syntax:

… CORRESPONDING type([BASE (base)] struct|itab [mapping|except])

Example:

Workareas contains the following data:

    L_workarea1 = VALUE line1(col1 = 1 col2 = 2).

    L_workarea2 = VALUE line2(col1 = 4 col2 = 5 col3 = 6).

Example 1: The contents of L_Workarea1 are moved to L_Workarea2 where there is a matching column name. Where there is no match the column of L_Workarea2 is initialized.

    L_workarea2 = CORRESPONDING #(L_workarea1).

Now the contents of the L_Workarea2 will have the following data:

    L_workarea2 =(col1 = 1 col2 = 2 col3 = 0).

Example 2: This uses the existing contents of L_workarea2 as a base and overwrites the matching columns from ls_line1.

    This is exactly like MOVE-CORRESPONDING.

    L_workarea2 = CORRESPONDING #(BASE (L_workarea2) L_workarea1).

Now the contents of the Workarea2 will have the following data:

    L_workarea2 =(col1 = 1 col2 = 2 col3 = 6).

In this example L_workarea2 is used as a based. This means that the contents of L_workarea2 cannot be overwritten. All other fields take the value from L_workarea1.

Example 3: This creates a third and new structure (ls_line3) which is based on ls_line2 but overwritten by matching columns of ls_line1

    DATA(ls_line3) = CORRESPONDING line2(BASE (ls_line2) ls_line1).

The contents of the Workarea3 will have the following data:

    L_workarea3 =(col1 = 1 col2 = 2 col3 = 6).

Example 3 has the same result as Example 2, but in Example 3 the data is populated into a new structure L_workarea3.

2. Summary

This chapter covered some of the important and frequently used new language features. This is only meant as a starting point for the more inquisitee developer and should be explored further. As mentioned earlier the new language features not only simply the code and reduces the number of lines but is also easier to understand.

Chapter 3: Core Data Services

Core Data Services (CDS) is a new data modelling infrastructure. With CDS, the data models are defined and consumed on the database rather than on the Application server. Hence, this helps in the code push down and drastically improves the performance.

This Chapter defines S/4 Hana and then goes on to explain what is Code push down. Then in Section 3 we cover the details of Core data services. The examples provided in this chapter are detailed and would help to get introduced to the new programming model.

1. What Is S/4 Hana?

SAP S/4HANA stands for SAP Business Suite 4 SAP HANA. It is a new product with a new code line for maximum leverage of SAP HANA. It is the next generation business suite and is built on advanced in-memory platform, SAP HANA, and offers a personalized user experience with SAP Fiori.

S/4HANA delivers massive simplifications (data model, user experience), innovations and offers personalized user experience with SAP Fiori.

SAP S/4HANA simplifies IT landscape and reduce cost of ownership (TCO), through:

- Reducing your data footprint
- Working with larger data sets in one system saving hardware costs, operational costs, and time

2. ABAP Programming model in SAP S/4 HANA

2.1 Introduction

The new ABAP programming model has been introduced with the ABAP release 7.50 SPS01, first only supporting the development of read-only Fiori apps, and then successively enhanced and improved with the following ABAP releases.

The new ABAP programming model is based on proven technologies such as Core Data Services (CDS) for the data modelling and access, OData protocol for the service exposure and the business object processing framework for the transactional processing.

The picture below gives an overview of the end-2-end stack:

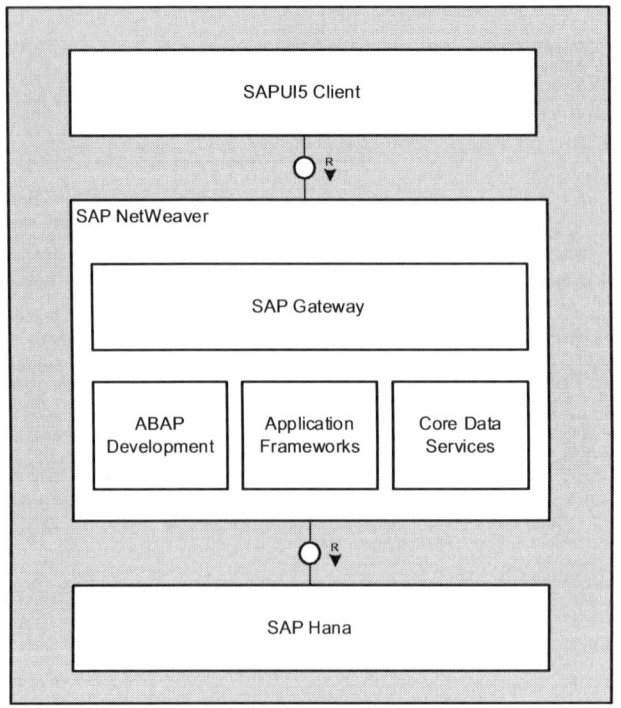

Figure 1: ABAP Programming Model for SAP Fiori

SAPUI5: this is the latest UI technology from SAP and provides Role based access.

SAP Gateway: SAP Gateway is an open standards-based framework that developers can use to more easily connect non-SAP applications to SAP applications. This is covered in Chapter 5.

ABAP Development: New ABAP Language and Development tools.

Application Frameworks: one of the most important Application Framewroks used in S/4 Hana is the Business Object Processing Framework (BOPF). This is covered in Chapter 7.

Core data Services: ABAP CDS provides a powerful data modelling infrastructure enabling advanced view building in the ABAP. CDS Views are covered as part of this chapter.

3. Code Pushdown

With the brand-new NW AS ABAP 7.4 SP5, SAP is adding new possibility for ABAP Developers to leverage HANA capabilities.

Code pushdown means delegating data intense calculations to the database layer. It does not mean push ALL calculations to the database, but only those that make sense. An easy example is if you want to add the balances of a customer's saving account. You should not select all savings account balances and add them in your application logic code. This can be easily done by summing the account balances in the database and just return the result.

In ABAP programming, Developers were always expected to have a layered development approach i.e. keep the business logic separate from the data base access layer. This lead to developers creating different Function Groups / Classes for Data base access and Application Logic. It might seem slightly strange that with Code pushdown we want to now put some Business logic in the database layer. But this is not new. Code pushdown was already being done in many different ways like using Count (*) in Open SQL or by using Stored Procedures.

4. Core Data Services (CDS)

With the availability of SAP HANA there has been a shift in the way applications are developed. The idea is to push the code to the database layer to get maximum performance.

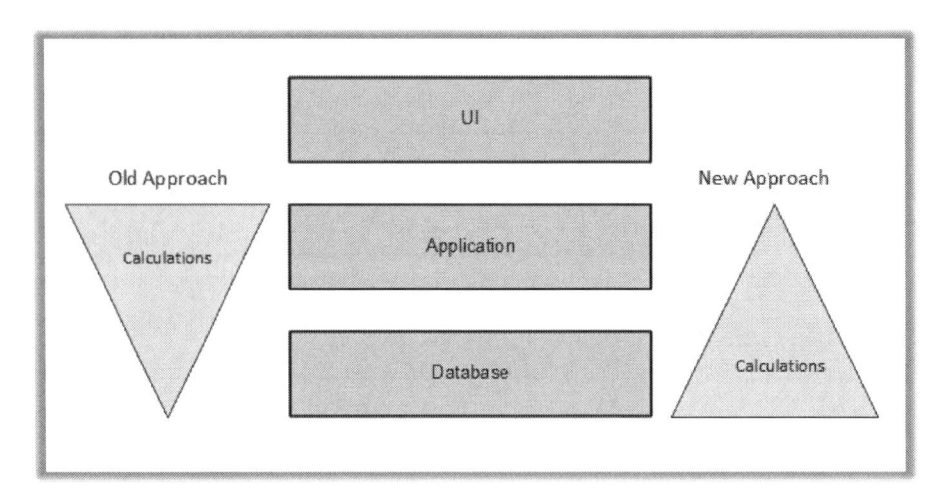

Figure 2: Code Push Down

To take advantage of SAP HANA for application development, SAP introduced core data services. With CDS, data models are defined and consumed on the database rather than on the application server.

CDS views are nothing but next generation database views. It can be defined for an existing database table and any other views or CDS views. It uses Data Definition Language (DDL).

CDS is an infrastructure layer for defining semantically rich data models, which are represented as CDS views. CDS allows developers to define entity types (such as orders, business partners, or products) and the semantic relationships between them, which correspond to foreign key relationships in traditional entity relationship (ER) models.

CDS is defined using a SQL-based data definition language (DDL) that is based on standard SQL with some additional concepts, such as associations, which define the relationships between CDS views, and annotations, which direct the domain-specific use of CDS artifacts.

CDS data models go beyond the capabilities of the DDIC, which were typically limited to a transactional scope. For example, in CDS, you can define views that aggregate and analyze data in a layered fashion, starting with basic views and then adding powerful views that combine the basic views. Another difference is the support for special operators such as UNION, which enables the combination of multiple select statements to return only one result set.

4.1 CDS Views: A Step-by-Step Approach

The steps for developing with CDS views are as follows:
- Creating a CDS view
- Coding the CDS view
- Consuming the CDS view from ABAP code

Please note that traditional SE11 views were developed using forms which had tabs for selecting various configuration settings, definition of fields etc.
In CDS based approach the view is created using code.

In the rest of the chapter we will create CDS views based on some of the most used templates.

STEP1: Start ABAP in Eclipse

First, you need to start ABAP in Eclipse and create a DDL source (CDS views cannot be created in SE80).
To start ABAP in Eclipse, open the Eclipse project explorer and switch to the ABAP development perspective.
You can create these repository artifacts as local objects belonging to the $TMP package.
To create a CDS view, right click on the package and select New -> Other ABAP Repository Object.

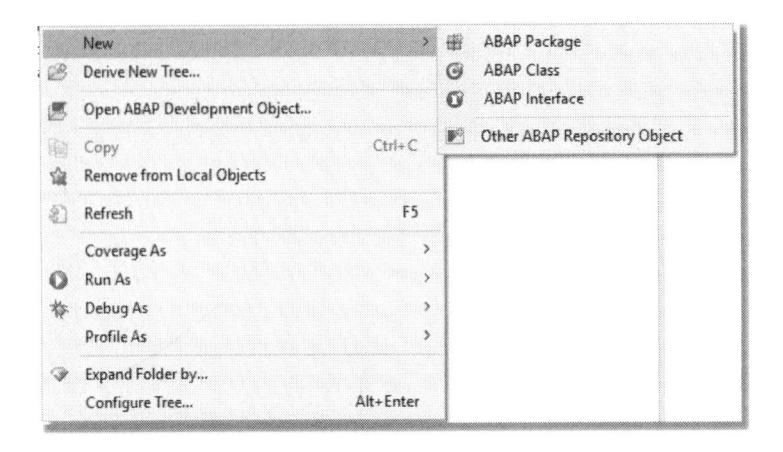

Figure 3: Create ABAP Repository Object

STEP2: Create a New CDS View

In the New ABAP Repository Object pop-up, search for the DDL source editor and select it to launch the New DDL Source wizard.

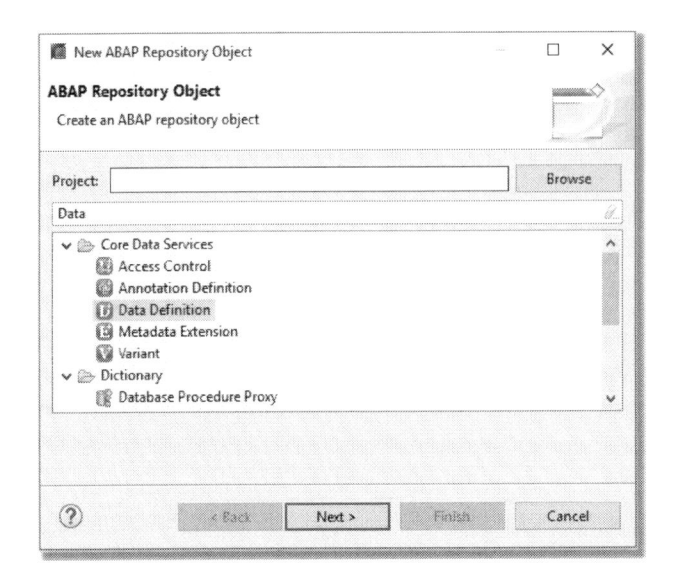

Figure 4: Create New CDS View

First, specify the basic properties of the view, as shown in Figure 5.

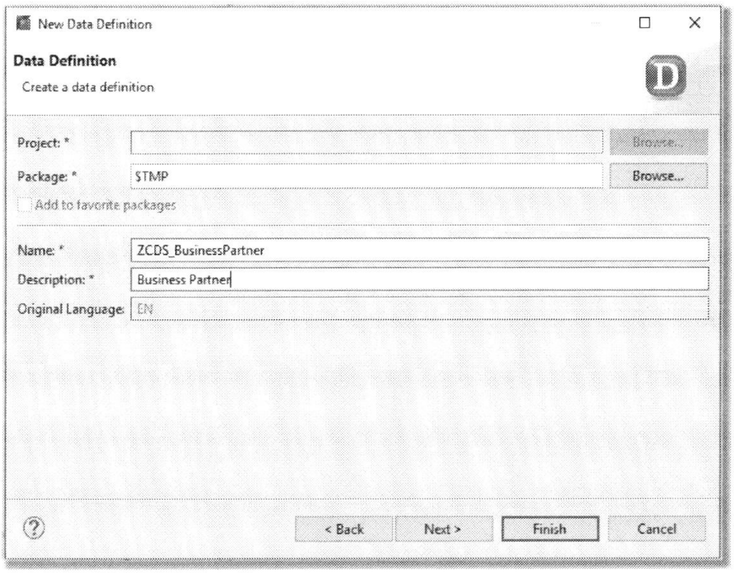

Figure 5: Create a Data Definition

Enter a name of the view and its description.

In this example we will be creating a CDS view to select Business Partners and its Default Addresses.

Since we are creating the view as Local object the system does not ask for a Transport request.

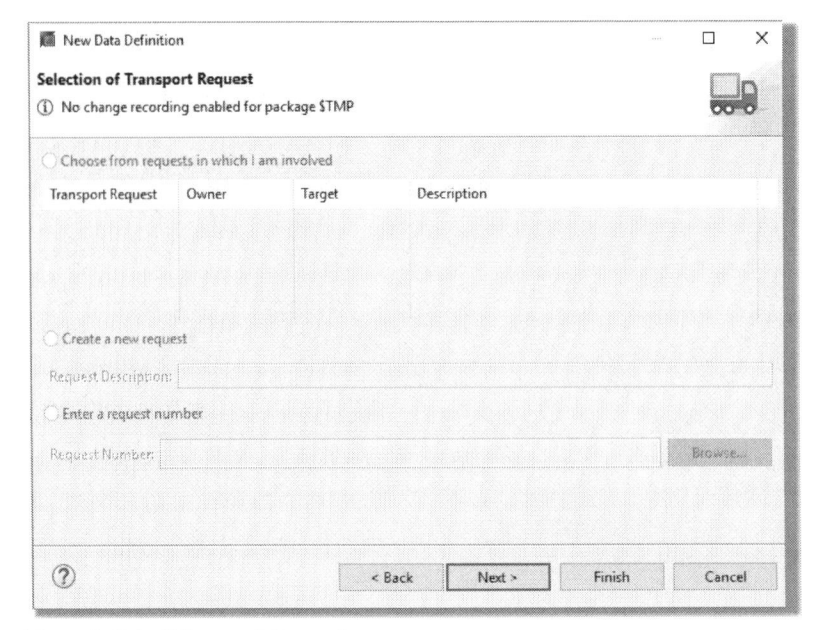

Figure 6: Select Transport Request

If the view were being created in a ABAP Package, then at this point in time the system would have prompted to specify a Transport Request number.

STEP3: Select a Template for the CDS View

The last screen of the New DDL Source wizard offers a selection of templates for creating a CDS view, including a display of the default syntax provided with each. The view can be created by either using one of the templates or without a template.

The templates include placeholders for code that you fill in step by step. If you later discover the need to change or extend the nature of your CDS view, you can always change the source code directly in the DDL editor and freely edit all parts of it as needed. This is particularly helpful if you want to copy portions of the source code from example code, for instance.

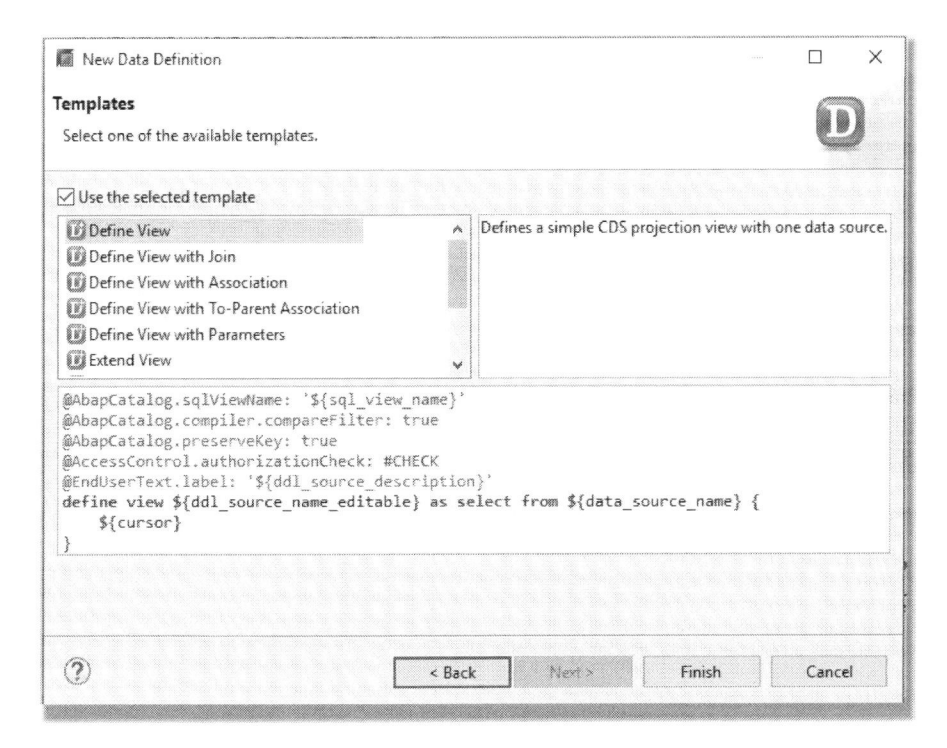

Figure 7: Select CDS Template

For our scenario we will create the view using the 'Define View with Association' template.

At this point let us understand the some of the frequently used templates.

- **Define View**: This can be used to read data from one table. This is like a select on a database table.

- **Define View with Join**: This is used to read data from more than one table. This is like a Select with Join to other tables. The table provides a template to join 2 tables, but this can be extended for more tables.

- **Define View with Association**: A View with Association is a type of join which is easier to write and understand.

- **Define View with Parameters**: CDS view can have parameters. The parameter values could be passed from the ABAP programs using the views.

- **Extend View**: This template is used when the CDS view is delivered by SAP and you want to extend the view with additional fields. E.g. SAP would provide a CDS view to read Business partner data. But this view could be extended with custom fields which you might have appended to the business partner table (BUT000).

STEP4: Complete the Coding for the View Definition

The code after having selected the Association template would look like as shown in the below figure:

```
@AbapCatalog.sqlViewName: 'sql_view_name'
@AbapCatalog.compiler.compareFilter: true
@AbapCatalog.preserveKey: true
@AccessControl.authorizationCheck: #CHECK
@EndUserText.label: 'Business Partner'
define view ZCDS_BusinessPartner as select from data_source_name
   association [1] to target_data_source_name as _association_name
     on data_source_name.element_name = _association_name.target_element_name {

     _association_name // Make association public
}
```

Figure 8: CDS Sample Code

You would notice that there are various placeholders which needs to be filled.

Let us examine each of the lines in the above code.
The first few lines of the view starting with '@' are called Annotations. After the sign @ the annotation describes a specific behavior.

The first annotation requires us to specify the SQL view name. When we had created the CDS view, we had specified the name of the view. But this was the CDS view name.
Each DDL source has 2 names. The CDS view name and the SQL view name. The SQL view name is the name which can be used to see the view using SE11.

@AbapCatalog.sqlViewName: 'sql_view_name'

Replace the text 'sql_view_name' with 'zv_bus_part'. A SQL view name only allows 16 characters for the name as for a DDIC table / view.

The template has 4 more annotations. These are described below:

- @AbapCatalog.compiler.compareFilter: true

    Defines the evaluation of filter conditions in path expressions of the CDS view

- @AbapCatalog.preserveKey: true

    Specifies the definition of the key fields in the CDS database view of the CDS view.

- @AccessControl.authorizationCheck: #CHECK
  Defines implicit access control when Open SQL is used to access the CDS view.

  #CHECK:
  If Open SQL is used to access the view, access control is performed implicitly if a CDS role role is assigned to the view. If there is no role for the view, a syntax check warning occurs.

  #NOT_REQUIRED:
  Like #CHECK, but there is no syntax check warning.

  #NOT_ALLOWED:
  No access control is performed. This produces a syntax check warning in

the DCL source code of a role for the view.

#PRIVILEGED_ONLY:
Privileged association (evaluated by SADL).

- @EndUserText.label: 'Business Partner'
  This is the description of the view which was specified when entering the attributes of the view.

Now specify the target data source for the Business Partner basic data. The underlying base table to be used as the target data source is named BUT000.

You can view the details of any of the syntactical elements that make up a CDS view definition on the fly by pressing the F2 key. The tooltip pop-up shows all the attributes, the corresponding data elements and types, and the associations (relationships) between the element and other tables or views, including their cardinality.

STEP 5: Add Associations details

While creating the view we had selected the template with associations as we wanted to select the default address of the Business partner.
We could create our own CDS view for default address or use the one delivered by SAP. In our example we will use the SAP BP Address CDS view (I_BPCurrentDefaultAddress).

The association could be added using the below code
association [0..1] to I_BPCurrentDefaultAddress   **as** _CurrentDefaultAddress   **on**
$projection.BusinessPartner = _CurrentDefaultAddress.BusinessPartner

Please note that the association requires the following information

- Cardinality: This describes the number of records in the Default address table for the BP. Since it is possible to have either no or max 1 default address, the association is defined as [0..1]

- CDS view name: This is the CDS View name of the Second table i.e. Default address table.

- Association condition: This specifies the join condition between the CDS views.

The current code would look like as shown below

```
@AbapCatalog.sqlViewName: 'ZV_BUS_PART'
@AbapCatalog.compiler.compareFilter: true
@AbapCatalog.preserveKey: true
@AccessControl.authorizationCheck: #CHECK
@EndUserText.label: 'Business Partner'
define view ZCDS_BusinessPartner as select from but000
association [0..1] to I_BPCurrentDefaultAddress    as _CurrentDefaultAddress
              on $projection.BusinessPartner = _CurrentDefaultAddress.BusinessPartner
{
}
```

Figure 9: CDS Add annotation

STEP 6: Add the fields for the view

Now we should add the fields which for the view. E.g. We would like to return the business partner key, first name, last name.

The final code would look like below:

```
@AbapCatalog.sqlViewName: 'ZV_BUS_PART'
@AbapCatalog.compiler.compareFilter: true
@AbapCatalog.preserveKey: true
@AccessControl.authorizationCheck: #CHECK
@EndUserText.label: 'Business Partner'
define view ZCDS_BusinessPartner as select from but000
association [0..1] to I_BPCurrentDefaultAddress    as _CurrentDefaultAddress
    on $projection.BusinessPartner = _CurrentDefaultAddress.BusinessPartner
{
    key but000.partner              as BusinessPartner,
        but000.type                 as BusinessPartnerCategory,
        but000.augrp                as AuthorizationGroup,
        but000.partner_guid         as BusinessPartnerUUID,
        but000.persnumber           as PersonNumber,
        but000.name_first           as FirstName,
        but000.name_last            as LastName,

    _CurrentDefaultAddress // Make association public
}
```

Figure 10: CDS - Add components

Once the code is complete, we need to activate the View (just like a SE16 view).

STEP 7: Display the results

The Eclipse editor allows you to execute the CDS views and see the results. The see the results, press the execute button

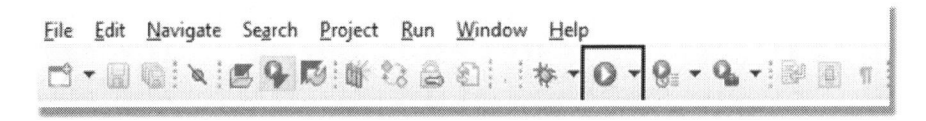

Figure 11: CDS - Execute

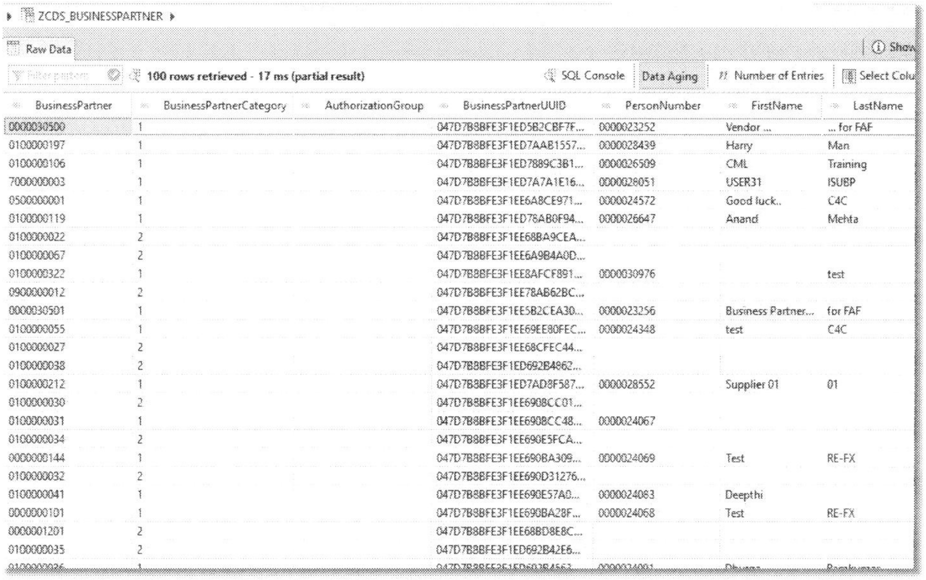

BusinessPartner	BusinessPartnerCategory	AuthorizationGroup	BusinessPartnerUUID	PersonNumber	FirstName	LastName
0000030500	1		047D7B8BFE3F1ED5B2CBF7F...	0000023252	Vendor ...	... for FAF
0100000197	1		047D7B8BFE3F1ED7AAB1557...	0000028439	Harry	Man
0100000106	1		047D7B8BFE3F1ED7889C3B1...	0000026509	CML	Training
7000000003	1		047D7B8BFE3F1ED7A7A1E16...	0000028051	USER31	ISUBP
0500000001	1		047D7B8BFE3F1EE6A8CE971...	0000024572	Good luck..	C4C
0100000119	1		047D7B8BFE3F1ED78AB0F94...	0000026647	Anand	Mehta
0100000022	2		047D7B8BFE3F1EE68BA9CEA...			
0100000067	2		047D7B8BFE3F1EE6A9B4A0D...			
0100000322	1		047D7B8BFE3F1EE8AFCF891...	0000030976		test
0900000012	2		047D7B8BFE3F1EE78AB62BC...			
0000030501	1		047D7B8BFE3F1EE5B2CEA30...	0000023256	Business Partner...	for FAF
0100000055	1		047D7B8BFE3F1EE69EE80FEC...	0000024348	test	C4C
0100000027	2		047D7B8BFE3F1EE68CFEC44...			
0100000038	2		047D7B8BFE3F1ED692B4962...			
0100000212	1		047D7B8BFE3F1ED7AD8F587...	0000028552	Supplier 01	01
0100000030	2		047D7B8BFE3F1EE6908CC01...			
0100000031	1		047D7B8BFE3F1EE6908CC48...	0000024067		
0100000034	2		047D7B8BFE3F1EE690E5FCA...			
0000000144	1		047D7B8BFE3F1EE690BA309...	0000024069	Test	RE-FX
0100000032	2		047D7B8BFE3F1EE690D31276...			
0100000041	1		047D7B8BFE3F1EE690E57A0...	0000024083	Deepthi	
0000000101	1		047D7B8BFE3F1EE690BA28F...	0000024068	Test	RE-FX
0000001201	2		047D7B8BFE3F1EE68BD8E8C...			
0100000035	2		047D7B8BFE3F1ED692B42E6...			

Figure 12: Display results

4.2 CDS Views

In the previous section we created the CDS view with Association. In this section we will create CDS views with other commonly used templates and understand its usages with examples.

The following Templates will be covered:

- CDS View with Join
- CDS View with Parameters
- Extend View

This section also covers how we can add Authorization checks for data access (via Data Control Language).

4.2.1 CDS View with Join

CDS views with Joins are used for reading access to multiple Tables / Views. It might seem as if there is no difference between this View and the SE11 equivalent. But there are many differences. A CDS view allows outer joins – something that is not available in SE11 database views.

The following options are available:

- Combination of Several tables (JOIN):

    o **Inner Join**: One row of the left table and one row of the right table are always joined to a common result row - provided that the JOIN condition is fulfilled

    o **Left Outer join**: One row of a table and one row of another table are always connected to a common result row - provided that the JOIN condition is fulfilled. In addition, rows of the left table without matching row in the right table are copied to the query result. The missing values (from the right table) are filled with NULL values.

    o **Right Outer join**: One row of a table and one row of another table are always connected to a common result row - provided that the JOIN condition is fulfilled. In addition, rows of the right table without matching row in the left table are copied to the query result. The missing values (from the left table) are filled with NULL value.

    o **Full Outer Join**: One row of a table and one row of another table are always connected to a common result row - provided that the JOIN condition is fulfilled. In addition, rows of both tables without matching records are copied to the query result. The missing values (from the other table) are filled with NULL values.

- Combination of results of several sub-queries (UNION)
    o UNION ALL vs. UNION
        - You can combine the result tables of multiple queries using UNION [ALL]. The individual results tables must have the same number of columns. The corresponding result columns must have compatible data types.
         If no name list specified, the column names of the result sets must match.

Let us create another CDS View with Joins. This time we will Create a View on the Business Partner table (BUT000) and Join it with Business Partner Role.

A CDS view with Join can be created using the Join Template.

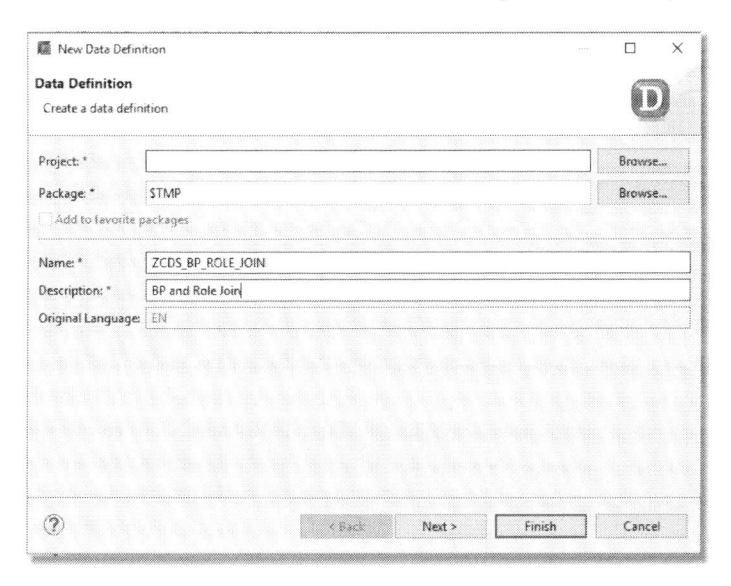

Figure 13: New Data Definition

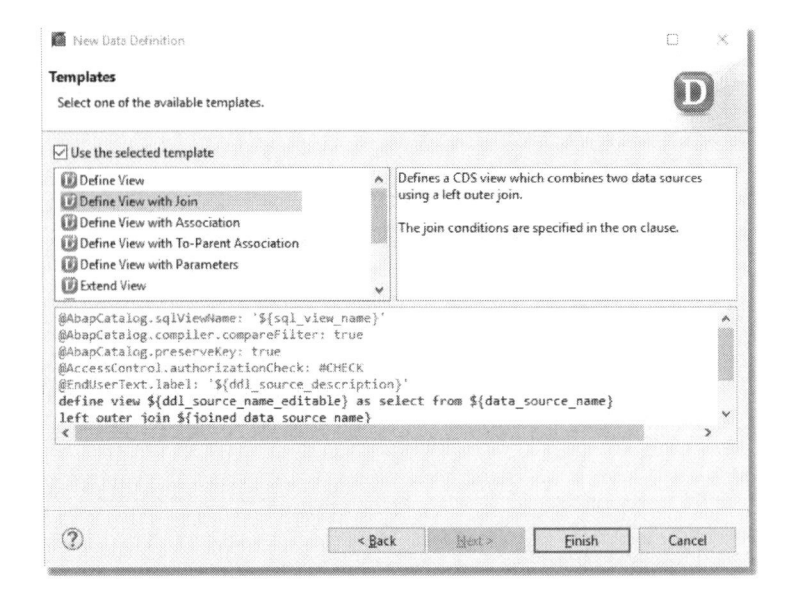

Figure 14: CDS - Select Template

The Generate code would be as shown below:

```
@AbapCatalog.sqlViewName: 'sql_view_name'
@AbapCatalog.compiler.compareFilter: true
@AbapCatalog.preserveKey: true
@AccessControl.authorizationCheck: #CHECK
@EndUserText.label: 'BP and Role Join'
define view ZCDS_BP_ROLE_JOIN as select from data_source_name
left outer join joined_data_source_name
    on data_source_name.element_name = joined_data_source_name.joined_element_name {

}
```

Figure 15: CDS - Sample code

As in the previous example, do the following

- Provide an SQL View name
- Enter the data source names.
- Enter the Join Conditions
- Provide the Fields for selection

After completing the above steps, the code would look like as shown below

```
@AbapCatalog.sqlViewName: 'ZV_BP_ROLE'
@AbapCatalog.compiler.compareFilter: true
@AbapCatalog.preserveKey: true
@AccessControl.authorizationCheck: #CHECK
@EndUserText.label: 'BP and Role Join'
define view ZCDS_BP_ROLE_JOIN as select from but000
left outer join but100
    on but000.partner = but100.partner {
    key but000.partner                as BusinessPartner,
        but000.type                   as BusinessPartnerCategory,
        but000.augrp                  as AuthorizationGroup,
        but000.partner_guid           as BusinessPartnerUUID,
        but000.persnumber             as PersonNumber,

        but100.rltyp                  as BusinessPartnerRole
}
```

Figure 16: CDS - Add Details

Execute the View and check the results

BusinessPartner	BusinessPartnerCategory	AuthorizationGroup	BusinessPartnerUUID	PersonNumber	BusinessPartnerRole
0000030500	1		047D7B8BFE3F1ED5B2CBF7...	0000023252	FLVN00
0100000197	1		047D7B8BFE3F1ED7AAB15...	0000028439	
0100000106	1		047D7B8BFE3F1ED7889C3B...	0000026509	TR0110
0100000106	1		047D7B8BFE3F1ED7889C3B...	0000026509	FLCU00
0100000106	1		047D7B8BFE3F1ED7889C3B...	0000026509	FLCU01
0100000106	1		047D7B8BFE3F1ED7889C3B...	0000026509	TR0100
7000000003	1		047D7B8BFE3F1ED7A7A1E1...	0000028051	MKK
0500000001	1		047D7B8BFE3F1EE6A8CE97...	0000024572	FLCU01
0100000119	1		047D7B8BFE3F1ED78AB0F9...	0000026647	TR0803
0100000022	2		047D7B8BFE3F1EE68BA9CE...		MKK
0100000022	2		047D7B8BFE3F1EE68BA9CE...		BBP000
0100000067	2		047D7B8BFE3F1EE6A9B4A0...		FLCU00
0100000067	2		047D7B8BFE3F1EE6A9B4A0...		FLCU01
0100000322	1		047D7B8BFE3F1EE8AFCF89...	0000030976	FLCU00
0900000012	2		047D7B8BFE3F1EE78AB62B...		FLVN00
0900000012	2		047D7B8BFE3F1EE78AB62B...		FLVN01
0000030501	1		047D7B8BFE3F1EE5B2CEA3...	0000023256	FLVN01
0000030501	1		047D7B8BFE3F1EE5B2CEA3...	0000023256	TR0803
0000030501	1		047D7B8BFE3F1EE5B2CEA3...	0000023256	TR0640
0000030501	1		047D7B8BFE3F1EE5B2CEA3...	0000023256	FLVN00
0000030501	1		047D7B8BFE3F1EE5B2CEA3...	0000023256	FLCU00
0000030501	1		047D7B8BFE3F1EE5B2CEA3...	0000023256	TR0600
0100000055	1		047D7B8BFE3F1EE69EE80FE...	0000024348	FLCU01
0100000027	2		047D7B8BFE3F1EE68CFDE1...		FLVN00

Figure 17: Display results

4.2.2 CDS View with Parameters

CDS views can be created with parameters which can be passed by the ABAP Programs.

e.g. you have a report with Selection screen. The user enters parameters on the screen and these parameters are directly passes to the CDS views to get the results.

The parameters are provided as Comma-Separated list with Type. The Types could be predefined type or Data elements.

These parameters could be used as ON conditions of JOINSs, Expressions in WHERE or HAVING clauses etc.

In a traditional SE16 view, the parameters used in Select can only be used to filter the result set, but here the parameters can be used anywhere in the CDS code.

Let us create a View with parameters to understand this View in more detail.

Those who have already started working on S/4 Hana would have faced an issue where they would have to access the F4 domain values to provide this as a Combo box in UI. This can be simplified by create a View which takes the Domain name as input, retrieves the domain values and returns the results.

To create the CDS view create a new with and this time use the Template with Parameters.

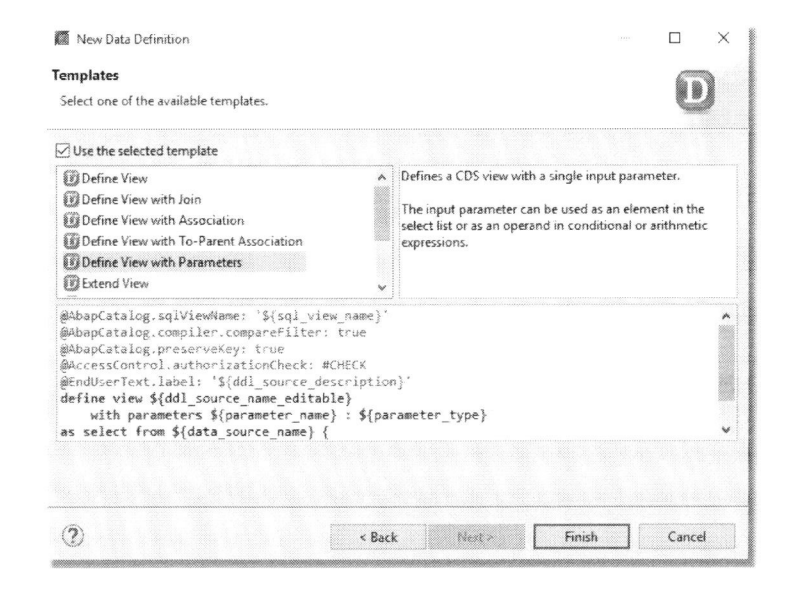

Figure 18: Select Parameter template

Now replace the template code with the details

The final code should look like as shown below:

```
@AbapCatalog.sqlViewName: 'LOANSWPDFIX'
@AbapCatalog.compiler.compareFilter: true
@AccessControl.authorizationCheck: #CHECK
@EndUserText.label: 'Loans Workspace - Term Value'

/*This CDS gives the domain values*/

define view C_Loanswp_DomainFixedValues
    as select from    dd07l as value
      left outer join dd07t as text on  text.domname  = value.domname
                                    and text.as4local = value.as4local
                                    and text.as4vers  = value.as4vers
                                    and text.valpos   = value.valpos
{
  key  value.domvalue_l,
//       @Semantics.text: true -- identifies the text field
       value.domvalue_h,
       value.domname,
       text.ddtext
}
where
       ddlanguage      = $session.system_language
   and value.as4local = 'A'
```

Figure 19: Sample code

Now activate and execute the view.

This time, the system does not display the results directly. It asks for the parameter value and then displays the results.

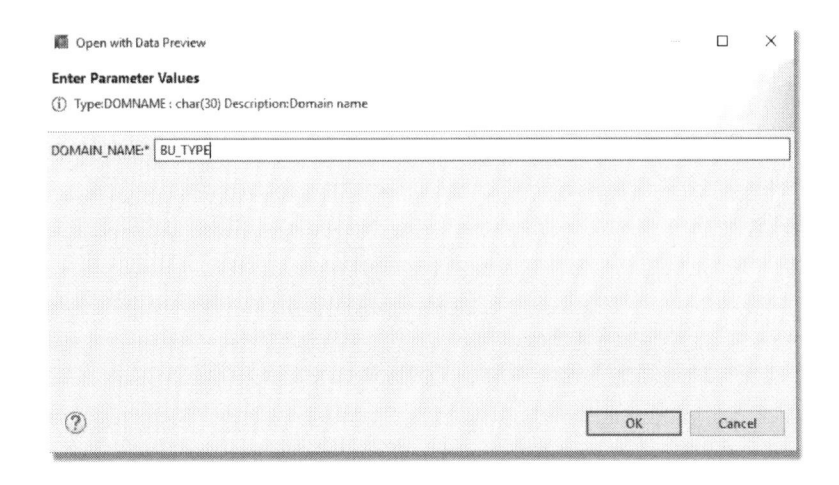

Figure 20: Enter input values

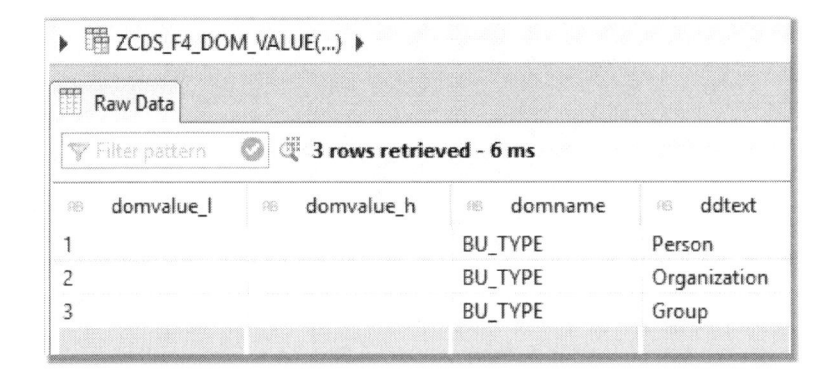

Figure 21: Display results

4.2.3 Extend View

SAP customers extend SAP delivered tables with Customer fields. E.g. An airline company would extend the business partner table to store the food preferences of its customers. Hence, the table BUT000 could be extended with new fields.

Hence, it should be possible to extend the SAP delivered CDS views with the custom fields as well. SAP provides this capability and the CDS views can be enhanced with additional fields, arithmetic & case expressions and literals.

The extensions are stored and transported in separate DDL source.

Let us create a view with the Extend template and understand the code.

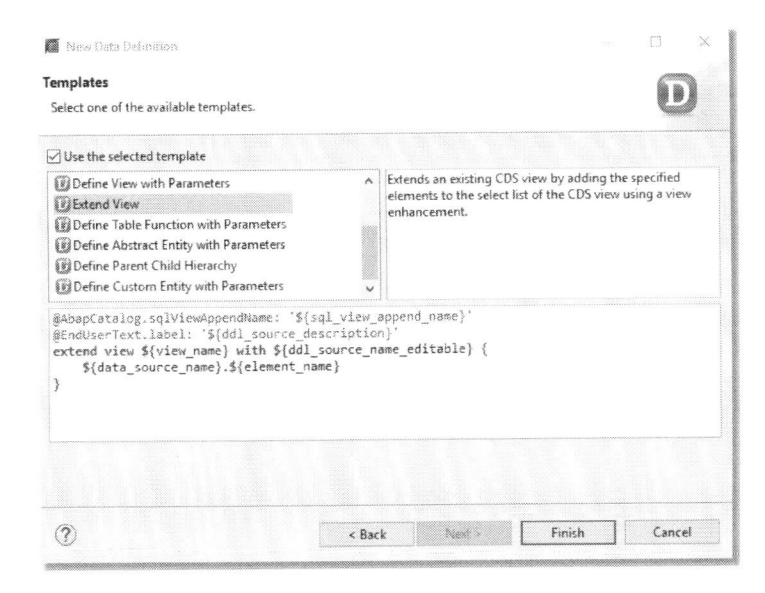

Figure 22: Select Extend View template

```
@AbapCatalog.sqlViewAppendName: 'zv_bp_extend'
@EndUserText.label: 'BP extend view'
extend view I_BusinessPartner with zcds_bp_extend {

  concat ( name_first, name_last ) as Name

}
```

Figure 23: Extend View Sample Code

4.2.4 Adding Authority checks to a CDS View

Just like in SQL it is possible to add authorization checks to the Views with the help of Data Control Language (DCL).

You might have noticed the annotation for authorization check in the previous sections.

@AccessControl.authorizationCheck: #CHECK

In this DCL approach, the authorization checks are executed as part of the view. Hence a CDS view is not only the DDL but it also includes DCL.

Let us assume that we want to create a DCL for the previously created CDS View (the one which displays the BP data).

```
@AbapCatalog.sqlViewName: 'ZV_BUS_PART'
@AbapCatalog.compiler.compareFilter: true
@AbapCatalog.preserveKey: true
@AccessControl.authorizationCheck: #CHECK
@EndUserText.label: 'Business Partner'
define view ZCDS_BusinessPartner as select from but000
association [0..1] to I_BPCurrentDefaultAddress    as _CurrentDefaultAddress
    on $projection.BusinessPartner = _CurrentDefaultAddress.BusinessPartner
{
  key   but000.partner                         as BusinessPartner,
        but000.type                            as BusinessPartnerCategory,
        but000.augrp                           as AuthorizationGroup,
        but000.partner_guid                    as BusinessPartnerUUID,
        but000.persnumber                      as PersonNumber,
        but000.name_first                      as FirstName,
        but000.name_last                       as LastName,

   _CurrentDefaultAddress // Make association public
}
```

Figure 24: Sample CDS View

To create a DCL create an Access Control object

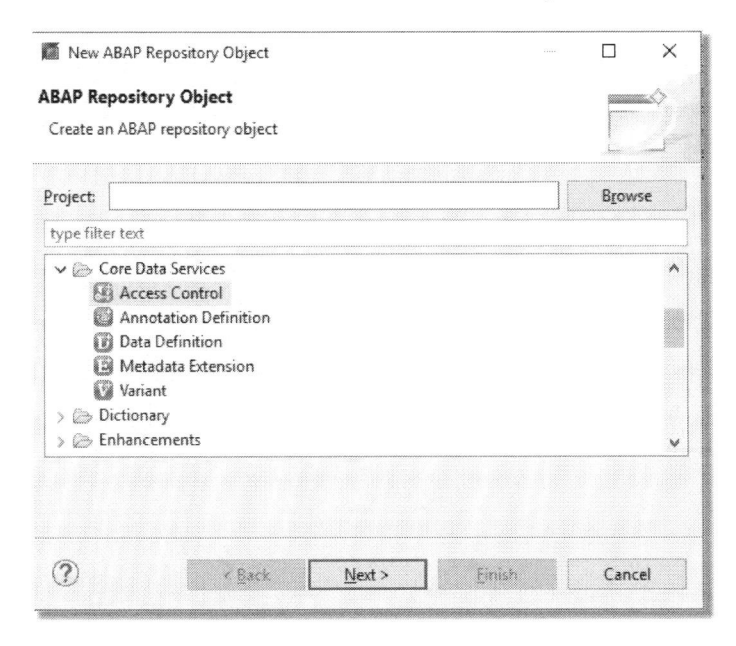

Figure 25: Create Access Control

Enter the below code

```
@EndUserText.label: 'BP authorization'
@MappingRole: true
define role Zbp_Auth {
    grant
        select
            on
                ZCDS_BusinessPartner
                    where ( AuthorizationGroup) ?=
                    aspect pfcg_auth ( B_BUPA_GRP,
                        BEGRU,
                        actvt = '03' )
                    ;
}
```

Figure 26: Access Control Sample code

Guidelines

- The DCL document must include the annotation @MappingRole: true.
- Only one mapping role definition per DCL source document is allowed.
- Other aspects than pfcg_auth shall not be used.
- Only one mapping role per CDS view is allowed.
- A DCL source document shall always include the mapping for one CDS view exclusively.

4.2.5 Using a CDS View from an ABAP program

CDS Views are used in the same way as the classical SE16 views. You could use the views in Select statements.

SELECT * FROM zcds_businesspartner INTO TABLE @DATA(lt_bp).

5. Summary

This chapter introduced you to CDS View and explained some of the commonly used Templates. With the details covered in this chapter you should not be comfortable in creating different views and exposing the data to the calling applications.
The next chapter would continue our journey and introduce you to SAP Gateway, so that you understand how the data can be exposed to the external world.

Chapter 4: ODATA

1. What is OData?

By definition, OData is "Open data access protocol from Microsoft that allows the creation and consumption of query-able and interoperable RESTful APIs in a simple and standard way".

What this means is that OData offers database-like access to the Backend resources and hence it is often described as 'ODBC for the web'.

OData is built on standardized technologies such as HTTP, Atom/XML, and JSON. It is different from other REST-based web services in that it provides a uniform way to describe both the data and the data model.

1.1 OData Architecture

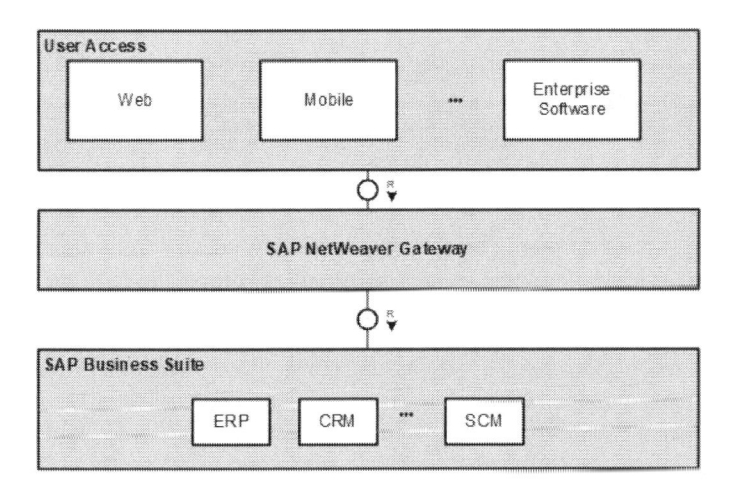

Figure 3: OData Architecture

In todays, fast moving technology world we need to access people-centric data in all kinds of devices. Hence, SAP NetWeaver Gateway is needed to empower SAP Business Suite to publish OData services.

SAP Netweaver Gateway enables consumption of people-centric SAP Business Suite data (content) for multiple channels.

In order to enable SAP Business Suite data to be consumed via the OData Protocol, we need SAP Netweaver Gateway.

The beauty of OData services is that they are multi-channel and are designed to serve many applications. You have one logical model that depicts how the users perceive the model behind the UI. Each separate UI provides a different view of the same logical model. Developers who know how to extract data from SAP systems should be able to find a suitable model that can be used by multiple application developers. Essentially, everything that is possible with the UI becomes part of the API.

The Gateway sits between the User Access (Outside World) and the Business Suite.

OData is an Open standard and can be consumed by any software that can communicate with HTTP and parse an XML document.

The OData service provides sufficient information to the consumer in terms of Metadata. Hence, it is not required for the consumer to understand the details of how the data is accessed and provided by SAP.

At this point you might think that this is like RFCs and Enterprise Services. But there is a difference. Other technologies used for communicating with the outside world were SAP specific but OData is an Open standard with wider reach. Hence it is easier to use and is understand more widely.

2. Gateway Service development

Gateway Service cannot be created directly by using code. These are generated using existing objects in the system e.g. Structures, RFCs, BOPF objects etc.

Once the Service is generated, these can be enhanced using the programming tools.

The remaining part of this chapter describes the creation of a Service using RFCs. Chapter 7 Covers creation of Service from CDS views.

2.1 Create Gateway Model using RFC/BOR Interface

The Service can be created using the Service Builder transaction, SEGW.

Step 1: Execute transaction SEGW and click on 'Create Project'.

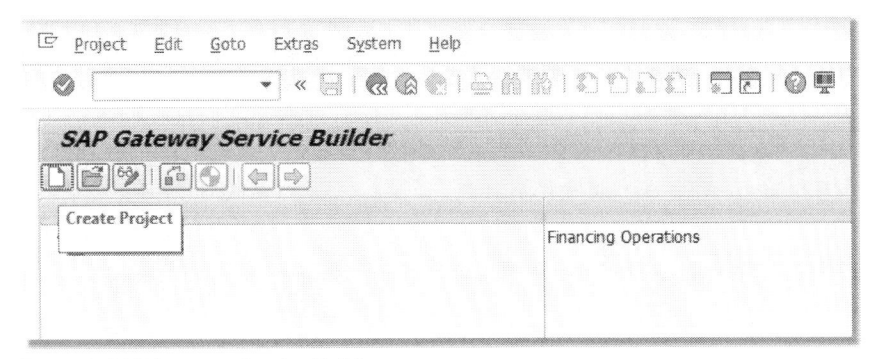

Figure 4: SAP Gateway Service Builder

Enter the name of the Project, Description and other details.

Figure 5: Create New Project

Step 2: Create the first entity by importing an RFC interface. For this right-click on *Data Model* and choose *Import -> RFC/BOR Interface*

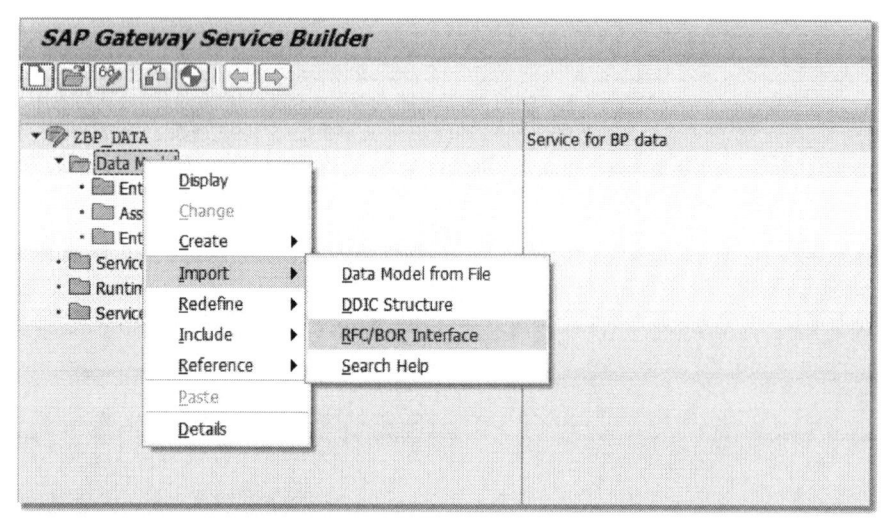

Figure 6: Import RPF / BOR Interface

Enter the following values in the wizard and then choose *Next*:

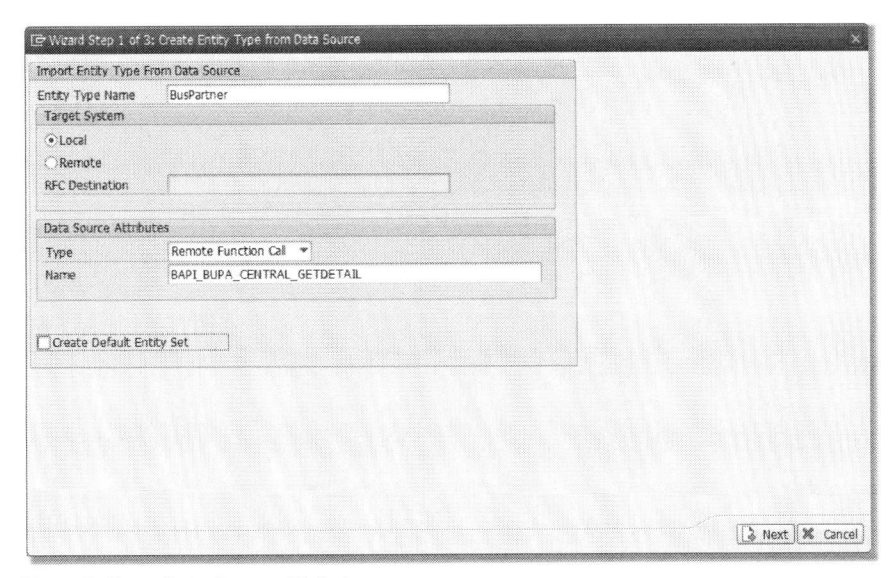

Figure 7: Enter Data Source Attributes

Select the entire data by clicking on the Checkbox beside the RFC name

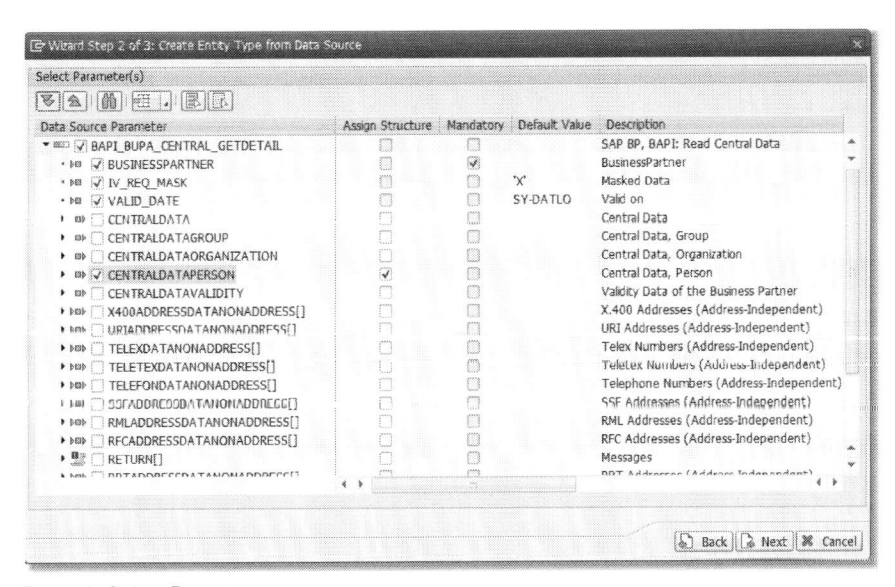

Figure 8: Select Parameters

Select the Business Partner number as the key and click on Finish

Figure 9: Select Key Fields

Save the Project.

Now the basic definition of the Model is done. As a next step we can generate the necessary runtime artifacts.

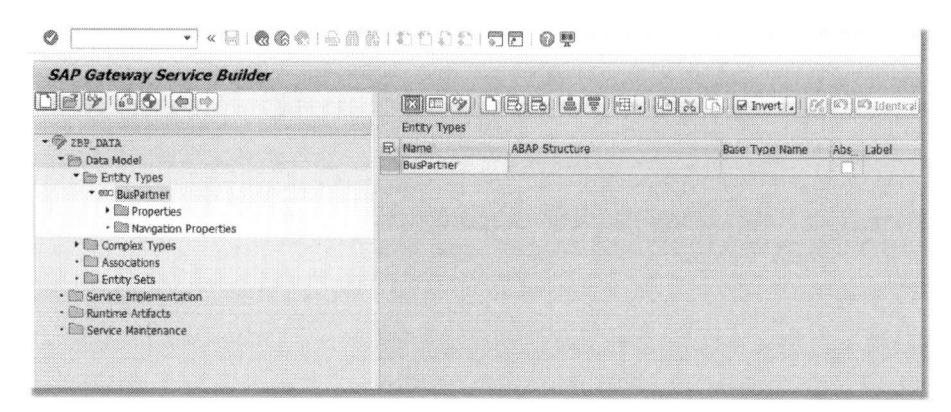

Figure 10: Created Gateway Service

Step 3: Choose the *Generate* pushbutton:

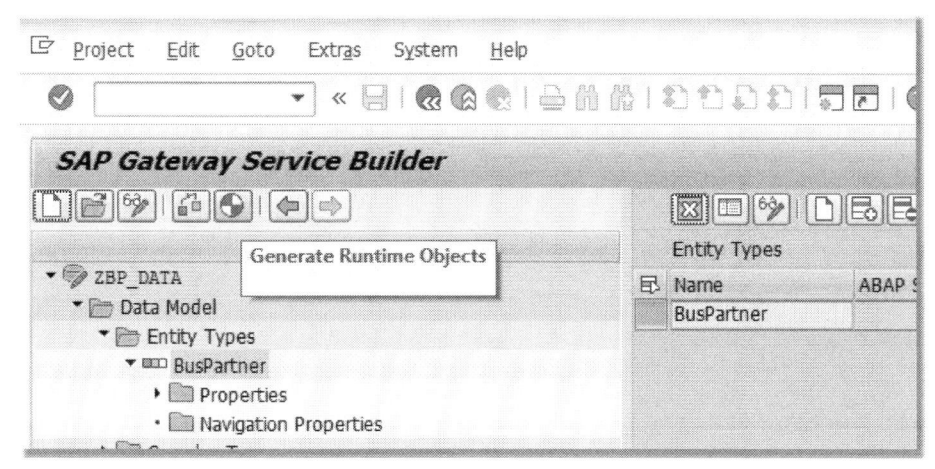

Figure 11: OData - Generate Runtime Objects

Leave the default values and choose *Enter*:

Figure 12: Model and Service Definition

Verify that the runtime objects have been generated successfully.

```
Messages
▼ ⚠ Runtime objects for project 'ZBP_DATA' were generated with warnings
    ▸ ⚠ Model binding
    • ▣ Model Provider Base Class 'ZCL_ZBP_DATA_MPC' generated successfully
    • ▣ Model Provider Extension Class 'ZCL_ZBP_DATA_MPC_EXT' generated successfully
    • ▣ Data Provider Base Class ZCL_ZBP_DATA_DPC generated successfully
    • ▣ Data Provider Implementation Class ZCL_ZBP_DATA_DPC_EXT generated successfully
    • ▣ Data provider base class ZCL_ZBP_DATA_DPC implemented successfully
    • ▣ Service ZBP_DATA_SRV was registered successfully
    • ▣ Model ZBP_DATA_MDL was registered successfully
```

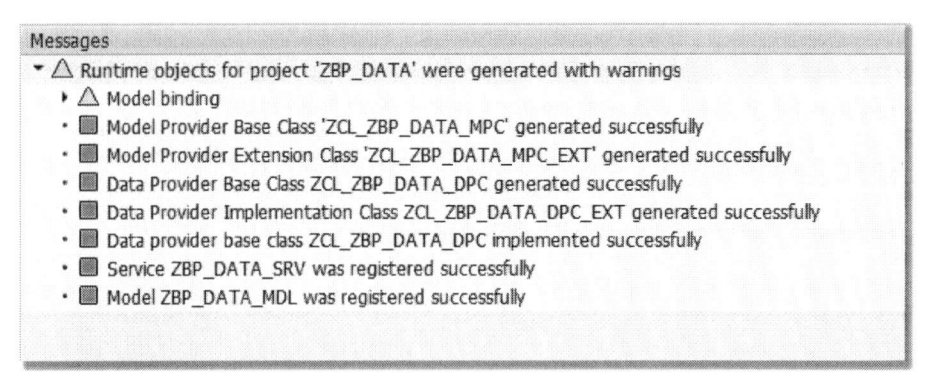

Figure 13: Service Generation Log

Now you would notice that run-time objects have been created, as shown in Figure 12.

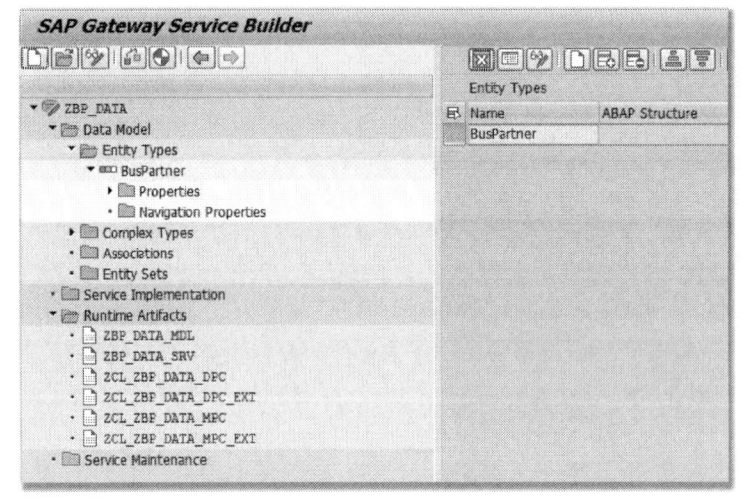

Figure 14: OData Runtime Artifacts

Please note that the system creates the following 4 classes:

- ZCL_ZBP_DATA_DPC: Data Provider class provided by SAP
- ZCL_ZBP_DATA_DPC_EXT: Data Provider class which can be extended by the developer
- ZCL_ZBP_DATA_MPC: Model Provider class provided by SAP

- **ZCL_ZBP_DATA_MPC_EXT**: Model Provider class which can be extended by the developer

Step 4: Now we can Register and Activate the Service.

The service can be registered either from Transaction SEGW or from Transaction /IWFND/MAINT_SERVICE. We will cover both the approaches.

a) **Generate Service via SEGW transaction**:

Double-click *Service Maintenance*:

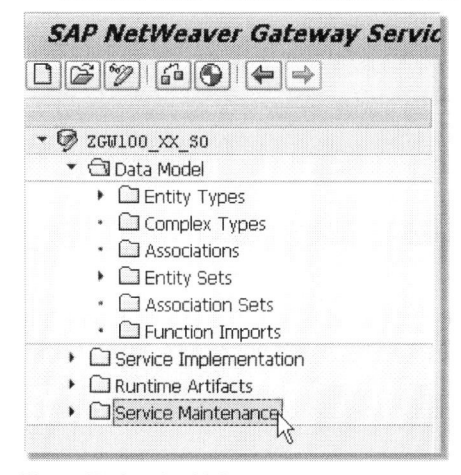

Figure 15: Service Maintenance

Click on the Register button to register the service as shown in Figure 14.

Figure 16: Register Service

Confirm the *Select System Alias* popup.

The next screen shows the 'Add Service' details where you could change the Technical name and provide a Package.
We would use the default values and enter *$tmp* as the package and choose *Enter* (Figure 15).

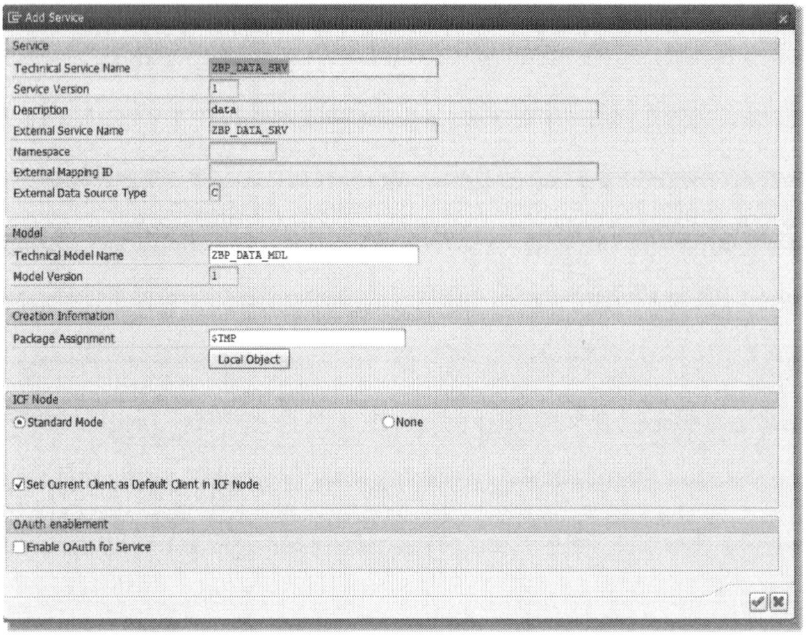

Figure 17: Add Service

The *External Service Name* is defaulted with the *Technical Service Name* from the Generation Step.

Verify that the service has been registered and activated successfully

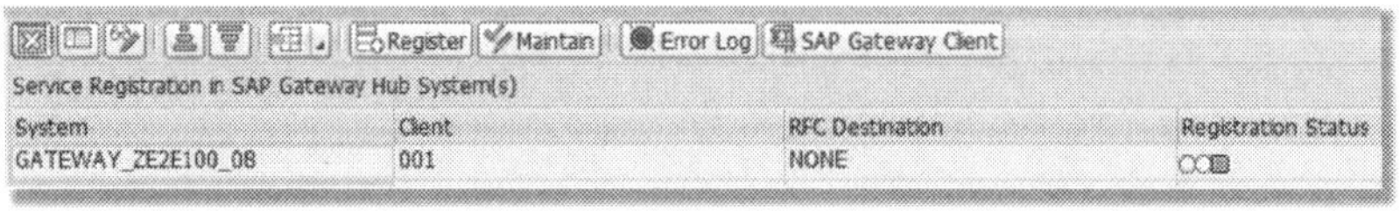

Figure 18: Registration Status

Now the service is created Successfully.

b) Generate Service via transaction /IWFND/MAINT_SERVICE

Execute transaction /n/IWFND/MAINT_SERVICE. This would show all the services registered in the system

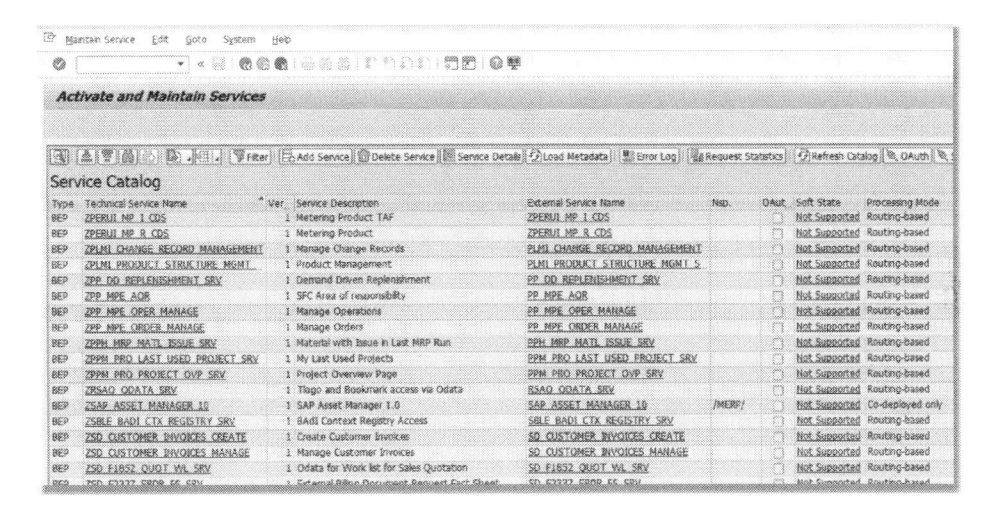

Figure 19: Activate and Maintain Services

To register a new service, click on 'Add Service'

This takes you to the 'Add Selected Service screen'.

To add a new service, enter the service name and click on 'Get Services'.

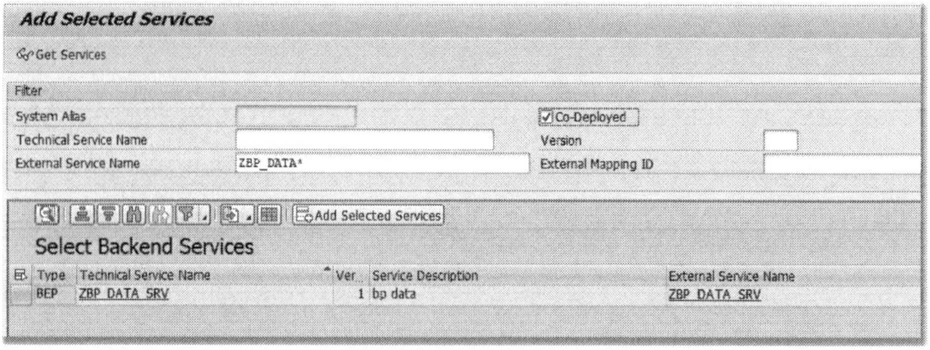

Figure 20: Add Selected Services

Finally, select the service in the List and click on 'Add selected services' screen. This then takes you to the 'Add Service' pop-up. Add the necessary details and click on 'Ok'

This has the same effect as creating the service via SEGW but this step requires you to search for the service before it can be registered.

Step 5: Execute the Service

To execute the service, execute the following steps.

Open a new window, start transaction **/IWFND/GW_CLIENT**.

Enter URI: '/sap/opu/odata/SAP/ZBP_DATA_SRV/$metadata' and choose Execute:

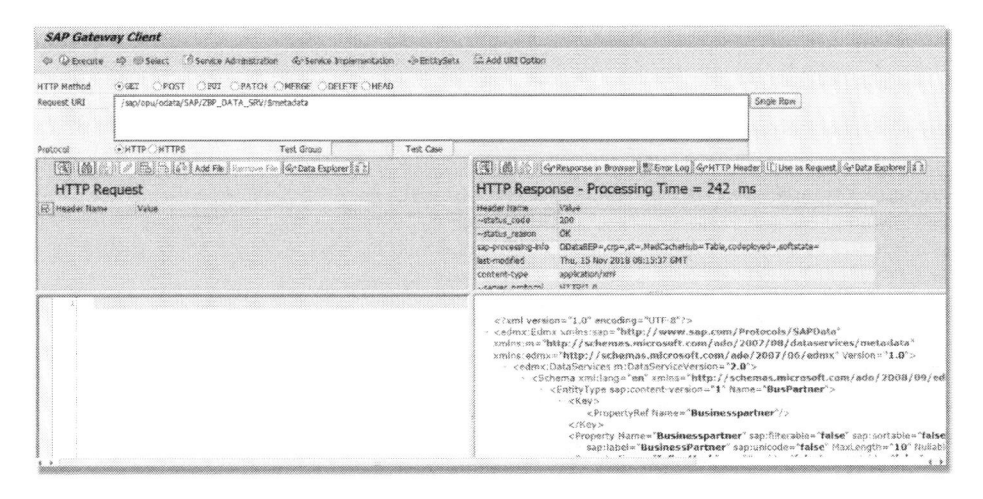

Figure 21: Metadata Response

The above figure shows that the meta data was retrieved successfully with return code '200'. Hence the service has been created and registered successfully.

Step 6: Add necessary ABAP code

Until now we have created the service and registered it. But we have not added any ABAP code to read or write data into the database.

Let us know examine the DPC EXT class generated by the service.

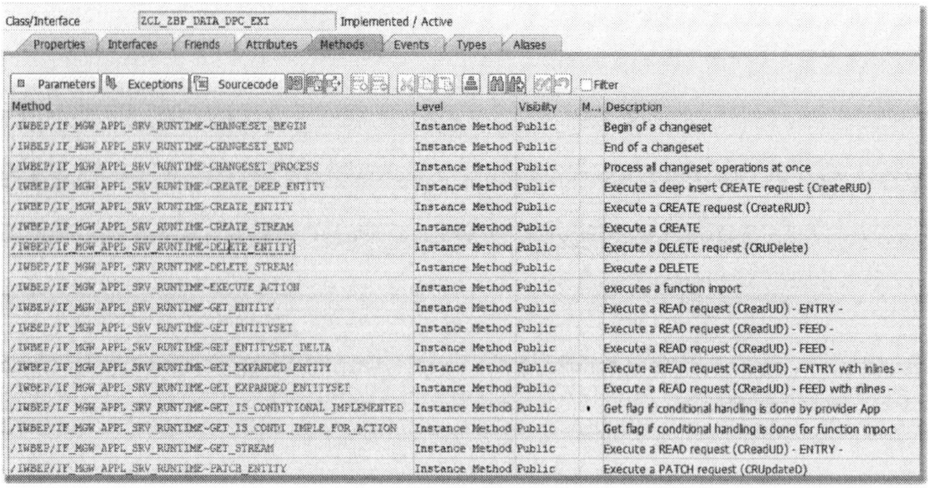

Figure 22: Diplay DPC_EXT class

The class provided many methods which can be redefined to write the CRUD logic.

For our example, let us write a logic to get the details of the Business Partner in the GET_ENTITY method.

Write the below code in the Business Partner Get Entity method.

The input to the method is IT_KEY_TAB which contains a list of values passed in the URI.

Since our Business partner field is the key field, we could get that into a variable then then use this to get the business partner details from the BAPI.

```
DATA: ls_centraldata TYPE bapibus1006_central,
      ls_persondata  TYPE bapibus1006_central_person.

  DATA(lv_bp) = CONV bapibus1006_head-
bpartner( it_key_tab[ name = 'Businesspartner' ]-value ).

  lv_bp = |{ lv_bp ALPHA = IN }|.
" Get the details of the BP
  CALL FUNCTION 'BAPI_BUPA_CENTRAL_GETDETAIL'
    EXPORTING
```

```
    businesspartner  = lv_bp
   IMPORTING
    centraldata      = ls_centraldata
    centraldataperson = ls_persondata
```

MOVE-CORRESPONDING ls_centraldata TO er_entity.
MOVE-CORRESPONDING ls_persondata TO er_entity.

Save and activate the above code.

Now we can test the service with the below URI in the Gateway client.

/sap/opu/odata/sap/ZBP_DATA2_SRV/BusPartnerSet(Businesspartner='131')

Please note: The BP 131 used in the above URI should be replaced with a valid Business partner number.

Execute the service.

As you can see from the below Figure, the data of the BP is retrieved and displayed in the Response.

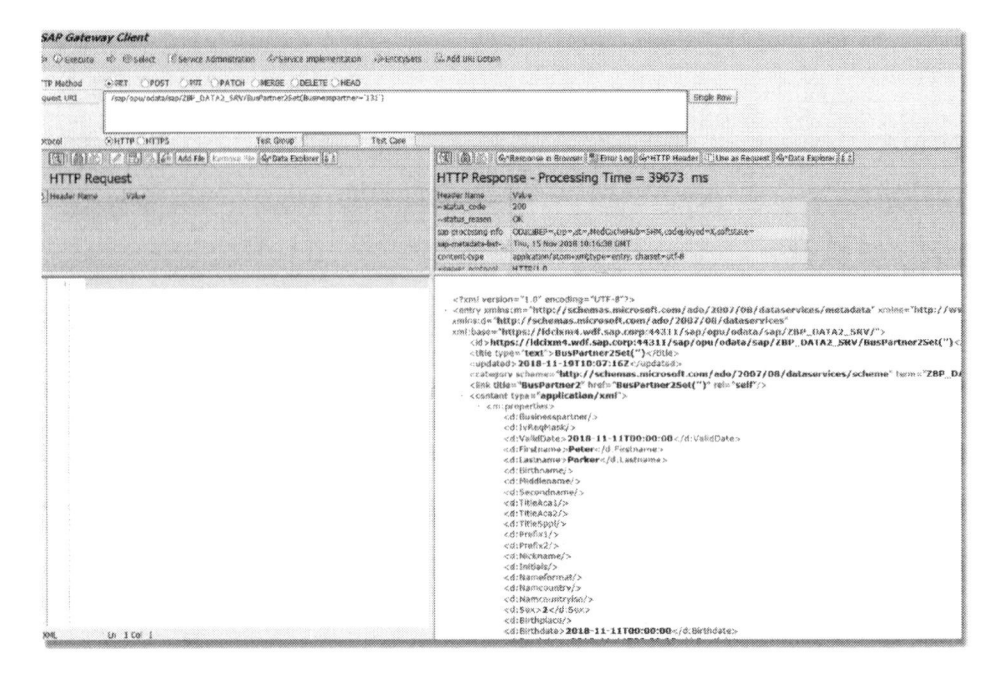

Figure 23: Retrieve data

Similarly, you could now implement the Create, Update and Delete Entity logic by redefining the methods.

6. Summary

This chapter introduced you to OData services and took you step-by-step through the creation of a Service via RFC/BOR Interface. With this topic covered you can now expose the SAP data to the outside world. This can now be displayed in Browser, Mobile, or consumed by any other application which can read OData. In Chapter 7 we will cover one more example where we will create an OData service via CDS annotations.

Chapter 5: Business Object Processing Framework

In Object Oriented programming, the real-world objects are modelled as Business Objects in software. SAP has represented real-world objects in ABAP in many ways in the last few decades with BOPF being the latest and the most accepted way of handling objects. It also comes with many advantages e.g. BOPF offers generic services like Database access, Transaction Process, status management etc. Hence, developers can now use these generic services to enhance the productivity and focus on writing the business logic.

In this chapter we will focus on the basic understanding of BOPF. This chapter does not intend to cover all the aspects of BOPF. The focus of this chapter is to enable an ABAP developer to get started with S/4 Hana programming and use BOPF for Transactional Processing.

1. Introduction to BOPF

BOPF is an SAP Framework for developing & maintaining enterprise business objects. It offers a set of generic services and functionalities to speed up and modularize your development to offer you ample flexibility to adapt your applications to your changing business demands.

BOPF is well established and broadly used within multiple SAP Business Suite and SAP ByDesign applications for e.g. SAP Transport Management, SAP Environment, Health & Safety Management, to name a few.

In S/4 Hana world SAP has chosen BOPF for Transactional processing and integrated it with CDS views and OData.

1.1 Business object Meta model

Figure 1 shows the BOPF Meta model.

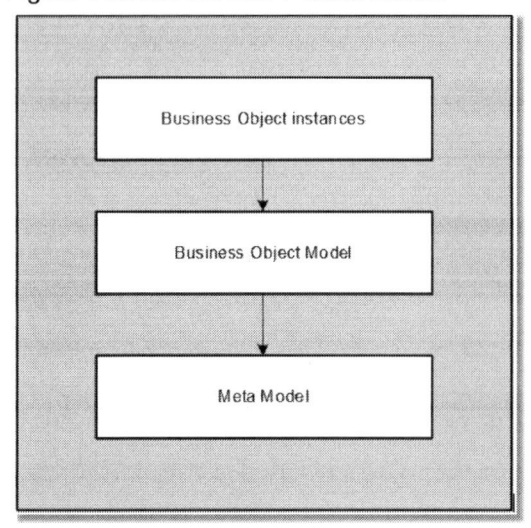

Figure 1: BOPF Meta Model

Business Object Instances: These are real-world objects created at runtime e.g. Sales Order, Purchase Order, Bank Deposit Account.

Business Object Model: Uses the components of the meta model to describe structure and behavior of a business object.

Meta Model: Contains Determination, Validation, Action and other model elements, which are necessary to model a business object.

The meta model defines elements that are used to describe a business object. The most important ones are shown in the Figure 2.

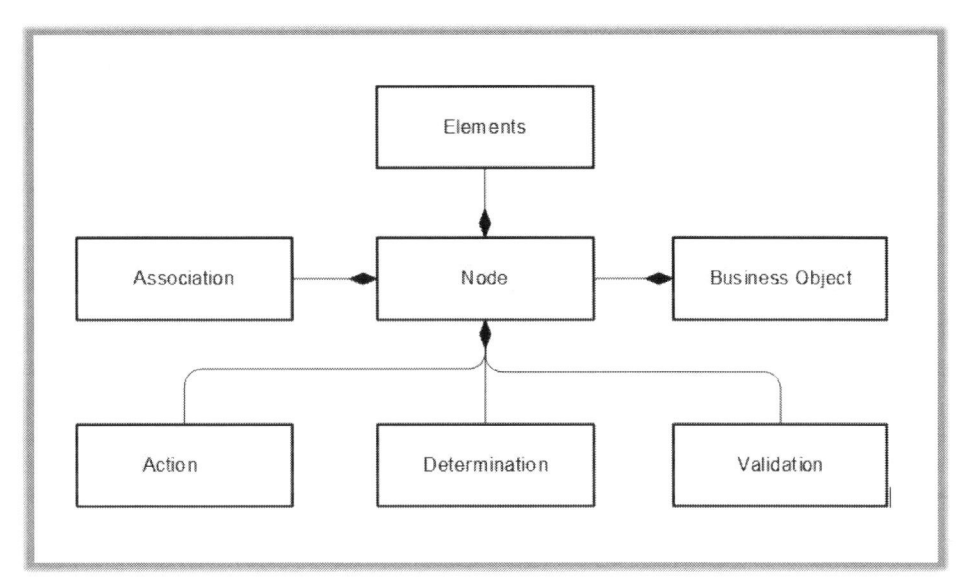

Figure 2: BOPF Meta Model

Node: A business object is a hierarchical tree of nodes. A single node consists of a set of semantically related business object data and the corresponding business logic.

Elements: Elements represent business information (e.g. InvoiceID, InvoicePaid).

Actions: Changes the business object instance. Is triggered explicitly by the service consumer.

Determinations: Changes the business object instance (side effects). Is triggered internally due to changes of the business object instance.

Validations. Does not make any changes on the business object instance.

Queries: Search for business object instances that fulfill certain search criteria.

Association Entities: Connect instances located on two nodes.

1.2 Nodes

A node is an entity of a business object that contains data and functionality.

The following are the main features of nodes:

- A node consists of attributes and can be instantiated at runtime. An attribute could either be a field which exist in the database table or it could be a Transient field.

- A business object consists of several nodes and each node consists of a set of attributes.

- The business object nodes are linked with associations to make up the hierarchy. The topmost node of the hierarchy is called the root node.

A Node Element contains the following:
- Associations
- Determinations
- Validations
- Actions
- Queries
- Alternative Keys
- Status Variables

Example:

The data of a Business partner could consist of general data like Name, Address and it would also contain Identification data. Since a BP could have more than one identification we cannot create just one node with both General data and Identification data.

Here we would need 2 nodes. One for the General data and another for the Identification data. The ROOT node of the BOPF object would be formed by the General data and the Identification Data would be a sub-node of the ROOT node.

When created in BOBX transaction, the node structure would look like as shown below:

```
Display Business Object ZI_BUS_PARTTP, Active Version

Business Object Detail Browser
  ▼ ZI_BUS_PARTTP
    ▼ Node Structure
      ▶ ZI_BUS_PARTTP
    ▼ Node Elements
      ▶ ZI_BP_IDENTITYTP
      ▼ ZI_BUS_PARTTP
        ▶ Static Properties
        ▼ Associations
          ▶ _BPIDENT
        ▶ Determinations
        ▶ Validations
        ▶ Actions
        ▶ Queries
        ▶ Alternative Keys
        ▶ Status Variables
```

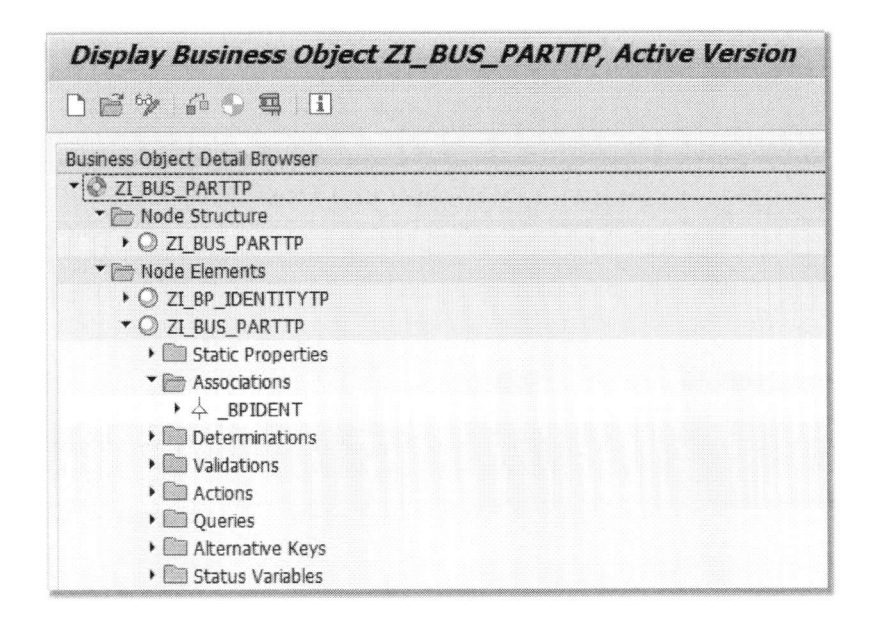

Figure 3: BP Example Business Object

In Figure 3, the Node ZI_BUS_PARTTP represents the ROOT node, ZI_BP_IDENTITYTP is the Identification node and these are linked with the Association (_BPIDENT).

1.3 BOPF Actions

Actions are used to implement certain operations on the Business Object. These contain Business logic and are assigned to Business Object Node.

Some examples of Actions are as below:
- Execute a Consistency check of the data
- Execute a Calculation and Display the details
- Send a Notification to the person responsible for the Business data etc.

These actions are not triggered by itself and must be invoked. These can be invoked either by
- by UI
- by another business object
- or by an action / determination.

Categories of Actions

In general, BOPF provides the following categories for actions:

- **BO-Specific Actions**
  BO-specific actions must be created explicitly for the node that requires a specific service implementation.

- **Framework Actions**
  Framework actions provide each BO node with core-services for which no implementation is required. They are automatically generated by BOPF when a node of a business object is created and are used internally by the framework itself.

A BOPF action could be added from the Eclipse by going to the Actions from the ROOT node.

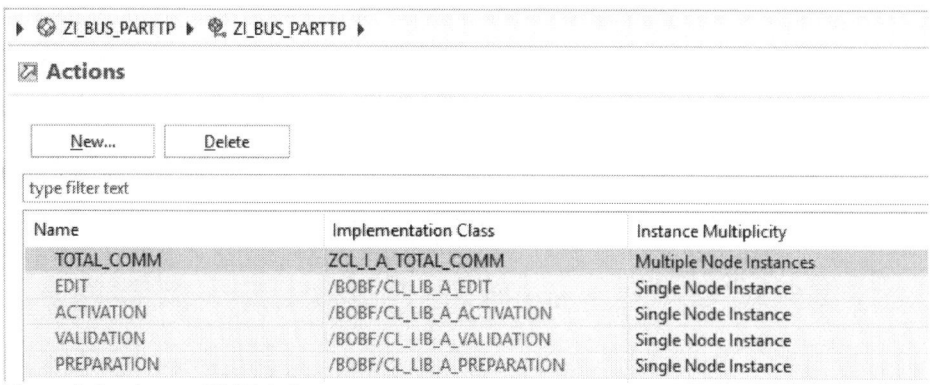

Name	Implementation Class	Instance Multiplicity
TOTAL_COMM	ZCL_I_A_TOTAL_COMM	Multiple Node Instances
EDIT	/BOBF/CL_LIB_A_EDIT	Single Node Instance
ACTIVATION	/BOBF/CL_LIB_A_ACTIVATION	Single Node Instance
VALIDATION	/BOBF/CL_LIB_A_VALIDATION	Single Node Instance
PREPARATION	/BOBF/CL_LIB_A_PREPARATION	Single Node Instance

Figure 4: Create new BOPF Action

Actions business logic should be implemented in the generated Action class.

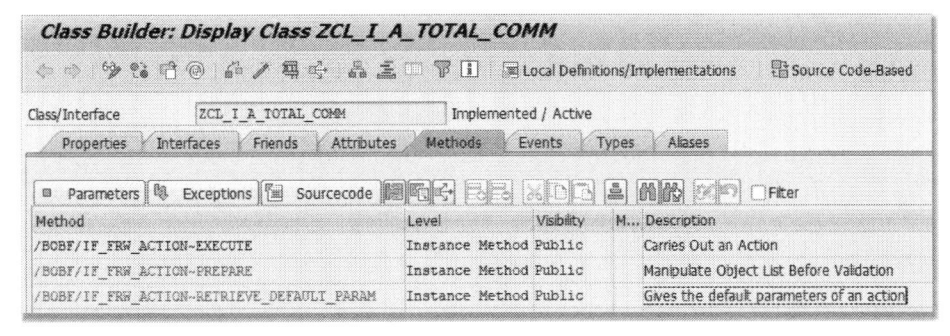

Figure 5: BOPF Action Class

The generated class has 3 methods:
- /BOBF/IF_FRW_ACTION~EXECUTE: This method should be implemented to add the necessary business logic.

- /BOBF/IF_FRW_ACTION~PREPARE: This method is deprecated.

- /BOBF/IF_FRW_ACTION~RETRIEVE_DEFAULT_PARAM: This method is deprecated.

1.4 BOPF Validations

Validations are business logic entities that are triggered in certain situations to check different aspects of a given set of node instances.

Validations, as the name suggests, is only used to check the data and not to modify it. They return messages and the keys of failed node instances.

A validation can be added from the Eclipse by going to the Validations page from the ROOT node.

Click on New Validations to create a validation and enter the relevant details. The system proposes the name of the class based on the validation name entered

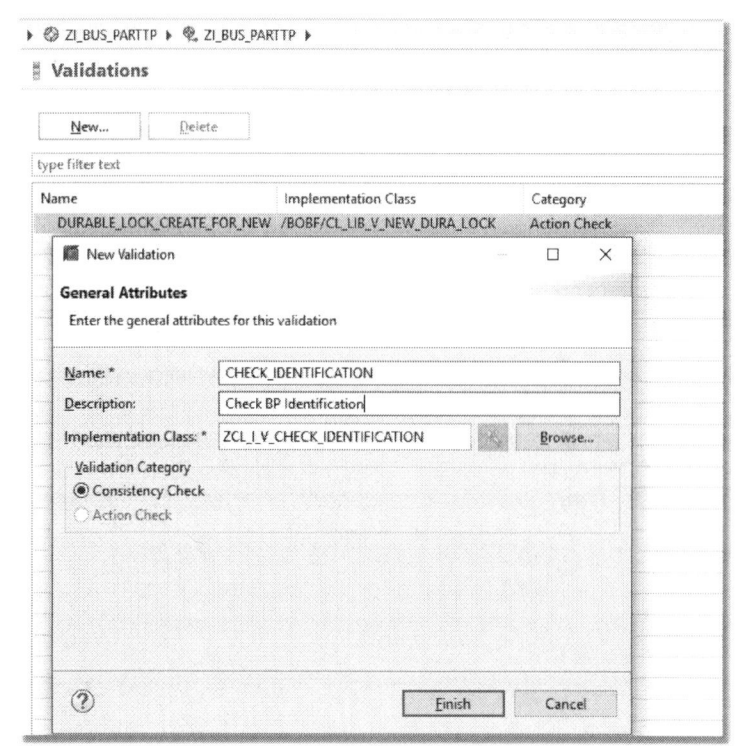

Figure 6: Create Validation

Once done, click on Activate to generate the class.

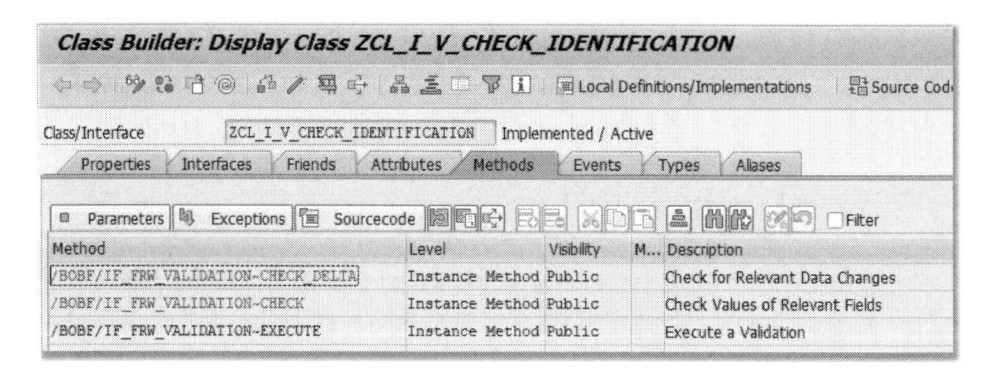

Figure 7: Validation Class

The generated class has 3 methods:

- /BOBF/IF_FRW_VALIDATION~CHECK_DELTA: This method was used to restrict the instances on which the validation would execute. This method is now deprecated and should not be used.

- /BOBF/IF_FRW_VALIDATION~CHECK: This method was used to restrict the instances on which the validation would execute. This method is now deprecated and should not be used.

- /BOBF/IF_FRW_VALIDATION~EXECUTE: This is a mandatory method and should be implemented with the validation logic.

1.5 BOPF Determinations

A determination is used to implemented side-effects of an action on a BO node. It is an entity of a business object node that is used to provide functions that are automatically executed as soon as a certain trigger condition is fulfilled.
A determination is triggered internally based on changes made to the node instance of a business object.

Example:
Let us consider a Business Partner create function. It could be a requirement to add the passport details of a BP whenever a new BP is created. Hence whenever a new BP creation is invoked an initial line for identification with the Identification type as Passport should be created.

To create a Determination, navigate to the Determination creation screen and click on 'New'.

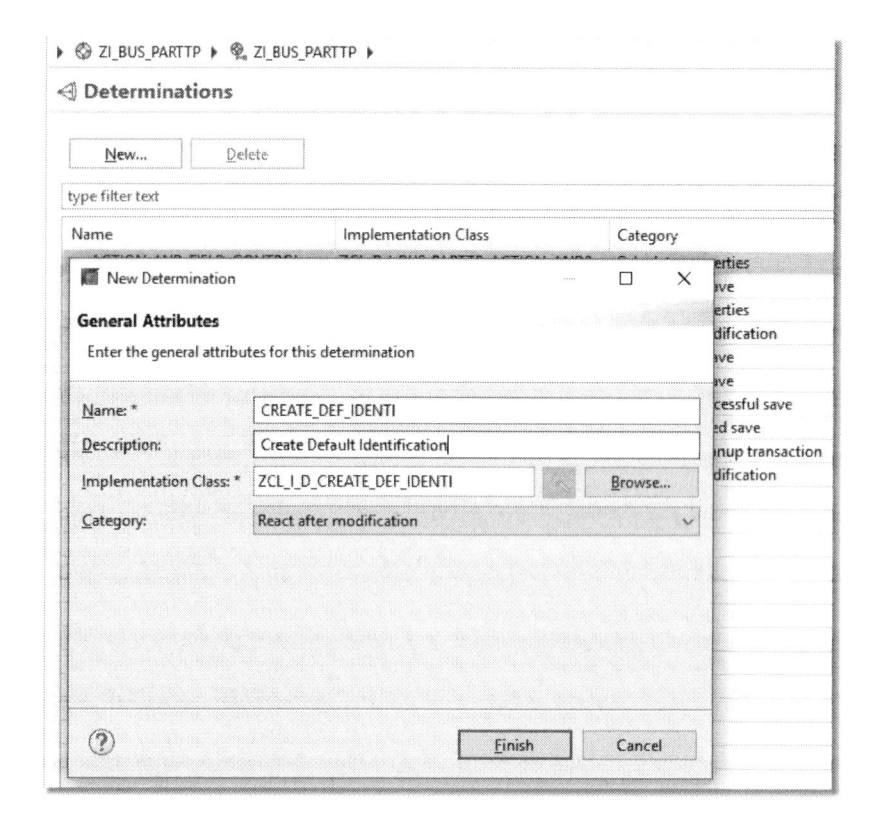

Figure 8: Create Determination

Once done, click on Activate to generate the class.

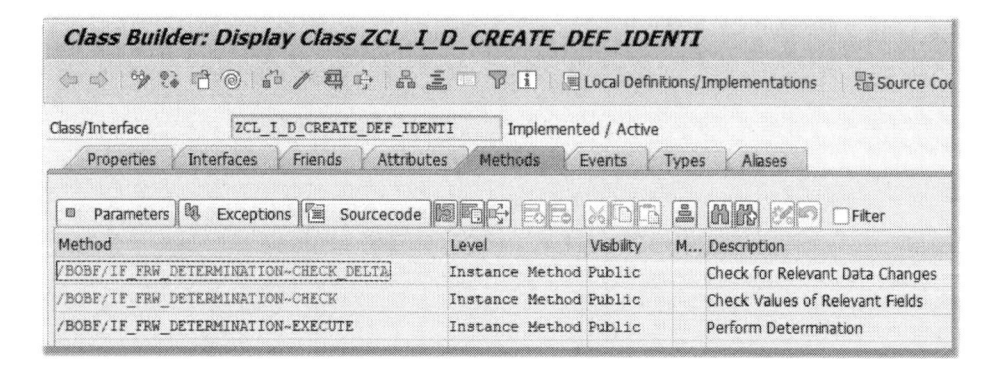

Figure 9: Validation Class

The generated class has 3 methods:

- /BOBF/IF_FRW_DETERMINATION~CHECK_DELTA: This method is deprecated.

- /BOBF/IF_FRW_DETERMINATION~CHECK: This method is deprecated.

- /BOBF/IF_FRW_DETERMINATION~EXECUTE: This is a mandatory method and should be implemented with the determination logic.

2. Creating BOPF Object from CDS views

Traditionally BOPF objects were created from transaction BOBX. But with the new Development paradigm, BOPF is integrated with CDS views.
If you were to create a new BOPF object manually, then ideally you would have to create the nodes of the object (e.g. Business Partner General data, and Business Partner Identifications – item table). Then you would have created an association and generated the object.
But if you remember from Chapter 4, the table and CDS Views already have this information. Hence there is no need to specify this again.

The BOPF object can be created directly from CDS views by adding the annotation -@BUSINESS_OBJECT. This annotation is an instruction to the system to create the BOPF object when the CDS view is activated.

3. Summary

In this chapter we saw how we can use BOPF for transactional processing in S/4 Hana applications. It is not necessary to use BOPF along with CDS Views. BOPF should be the Framework of choice for processing of real-world objects.

With this chapter we have covered the key components of a S/4 Hana architecture.
You should now be able to create end-to-end application successfully.
To further guide the developers, the next chapter provided a step-by-step guide to create a Draft based business application.

Chapter 6: Exercise - Building a draft-enabled business object

We have always come across situations where we accidently terminate our session by closing the Browser or we lose data when the server crashes. The result is same - the data entered in the screen is lost and the user must manually input the lost data again!

Now consider a similar situation when working on a document (e.g. Word) and the system crashes. The data entered between the last save and the current version could have been lost if we did not have any recovery mechanism.

Let us take the problem to an Enterprise application. The thought that the data could be lost and must be entered again would already cause some nervousness among the users. Creating a Contract in ERP requires entering lots of data including sensitive data like amounts, quantities etc. These must be verified and re-verified before the Contract is finalized. Hence loosing this data before this is saved causes lot of rework. The solution to this problem is to use Draft-Enabled Business Object.

A draft is an interim version of an entity that is not saved in the active version of the data. Draft is an auto-save feature which saves the data in a separate set of tables (called Draft tables) whenever the users adds or changes information within a business entity.

In SAP Fiori, drafts data provides the following advantages:

- To keep unsaved changes if an editing activity is interrupted, allowing users to resume editing later.
- To prevent data loss if an app terminates unexpectedly.
- As a locking mechanism to prevent multiple users from editing the same object concurrently.

Such an app must always be able to deal with two versions of data:

- The **active data** that represents the state of the business entity that is stored in the active persistence.

- The **draft data** that represents the transient state of a business entity until it is permanently stored in the persistence layer as active data.

Draft Types

There are different types of Draft which can be chosen based on the scenario:

- **Exclusive Draft**: Here the exclusive draft document is created by the user who is the only processor. In this case, per business entity an active document instance may have no or just one exclusive edit draft document. Therefore, a non-expired edit draft document blocks other users from editing the active document.

- **Shared Draft**: The shared draft document is created by the owner who may also be one of the processors. Further users are either admitted by actively inviting them (e.g. by the owner) to access the draft document or by automatically granting them access through responsibility or business configuration.

- **Collaborative Draft**: The collaborative draft document is created by the owner who may also be one of the processors. Further authorized users are either admitted by actively inviting them to access the draft document (e.g. by the owner) or by automatically granting them access through responsibility or business configuration.

1. Scenario

The aim of this exercise if to create an end-to-end Draft-enabled custom application. We will use most of the tools / technologies we have covered in this book i.e. CDS views. BOPF, OData etc.

Let us create a Business partner application which will allows us to create new Business Partners in the system. The user will be able to enter the Business Partner basic data and Identification data.

The data model for the application would be as below:

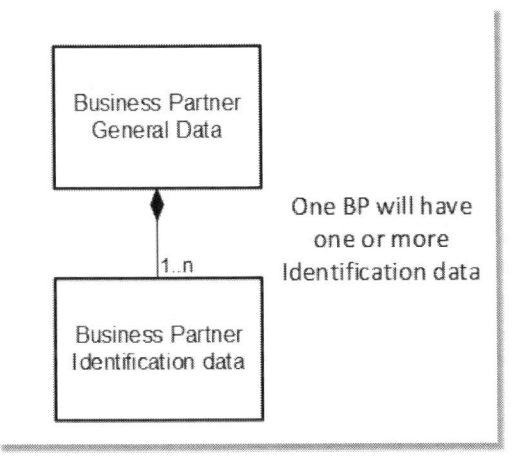

Figure 1: Business Partner Entity diagram

The exercise follows a bottom-up approach and starts with the creation of the tables for storing the BP data. It then covers the creation of CDS views followed by BOPF object and the OData service.

This exercise is designed in a way that it can be followed easily and gives an overall view of how the concepts discussed in this book come together to create a good application.

1.1 Create a Base table for BP header and Identification data

Let us first create Database tables for the Business Partner General data using SE11 transaction. Enter the table name as ZBUS_PART. The table can also be created using Eclipse.

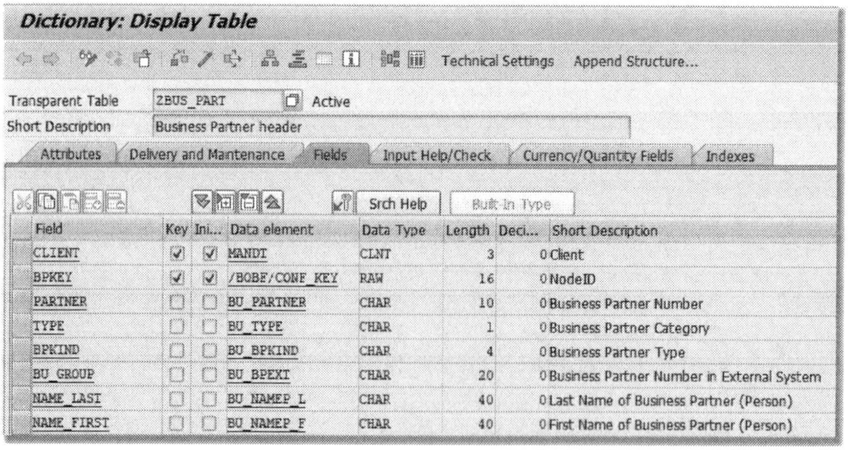

Field	Key	Ini...	Data element	Data Type	Length	Deci...	Short Description
CLIENT	☑	☑	MANDT	CLNT	3	0	Client
BPKEY	☑	☑	/BOBF/CONF_KEY	RAW	16	0	NodeID
PARTNER	☐	☐	BU_PARTNER	CHAR	10	0	Business Partner Number
TYPE	☐	☐	BU_TYPE	CHAR	1	0	Business Partner Category
BPKIND	☐	☐	BU_BPKIND	CHAR	4	0	Business Partner Type
BU_GROUP	☐	☐	BU_BPEXT	CHAR	20	0	Business Partner Number in External System
NAME_LAST	☐	☐	BU_NAMEP_L	CHAR	40	0	Last Name of Business Partner (Person)
NAME_FIRST	☐	☐	BU_NAMEP_F	CHAR	40	0	First Name of Business Partner (Person)

Figure 2: Display Business Partner table

Please note that in a traditional database table, the keys of the table would be the data which forms the Key. But in the BOPF world, the key is a GUID (32 Characters long).

The code in Eclipse editor for the table would be as shown below:

```
@EndUserText.label : 'Business Partner header'
@AbapCatalog.enhancementCategory : #NOT_CLASSIFIED
@AbapCatalog.tableCategory : #TRANSPARENT
@AbapCatalog.deliveryClass : #A
@AbapCatalog.dataMaintenance : #LIMITED
define table zbus_part {
  key client : mandt not null;
  key bpkey  : /bobf/conf_key not null;
  partner    : bu_partner;
  type       : bu_type;
  bpkind     : bu_bpkind;
  bu_group   : bu_bpext;
  name_last  : bu_namep_l;
  name_first : bu_namep_f;

    }
```

Now let us create a table for Storing Business Partner Identification data – ZBP_IDENTITY

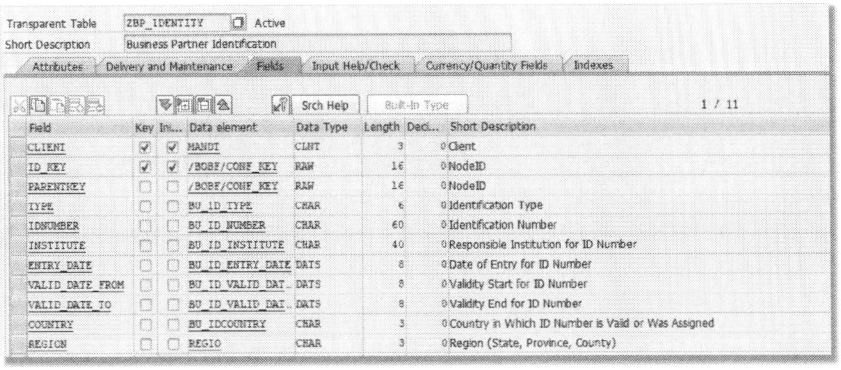

[Figure: Screenshot of SAP Transparent Table ZBP_IDENTITY showing fields CLIENT, ID_KEY, PARENTKEY, TYPE, IDNUMBER, INSTITUTE, ENTRY_DATE, VALID_DATE_FROM, VALID_DATE_TO, COUNTRY, REGION]

Figure 3: Display Partner Identification table

The code in Eclipse would be as follows:

```
@EndUserText.label : 'Business Partner Identification'
@AbapCatalog.enhancementCategory : #NOT_CLASSIFIED
@AbapCatalog.tableCategory : #TRANSPARENT
@AbapCatalog.deliveryClass : #A
@AbapCatalog.dataMaintenance : #LIMITED
define table zbp_identity {
  key client      : mandt not null;
  key id_key      : /bobf/conf_key not null;
  parentkey       : /bobf/conf_key;
  type            : bu_id_type;
  idnumber        : bu_id_number;
  institute       : bu_id_institute;
  entry_date      : bu_id_entry_date;
  valid_date_from : bu_id_valid_date_from;
  valid_date_to   : bu_id_valid_date_to;
  country         : bu_idcountry;
  region          : regio;

}
```

1.2 Create the Interface View for the base tables

The interface view is intended to expose the required fields of the table and rename them (if required) to make them semantically more meaningful. In this section we will create Basic and Interface views for the tables created in Section 2.

Create a new data definition file (under Core data services)

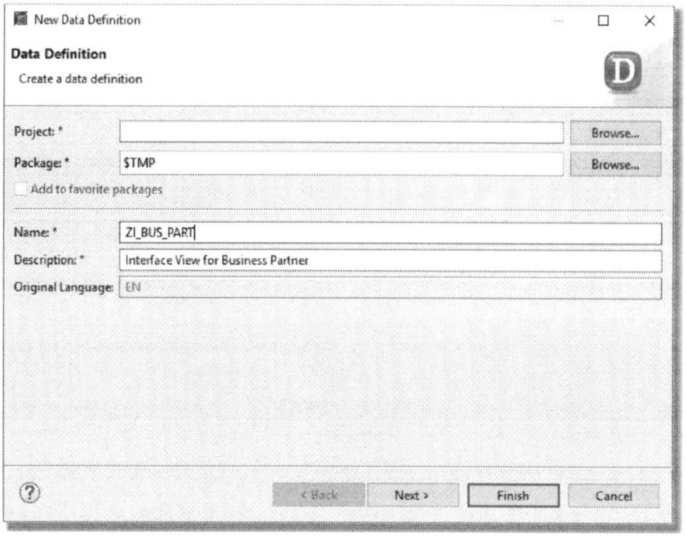

Figure 4: Create Business Partner Data definition

Select the 'Define View' Template and click on Finish.

The generated code is as shown below:

```
@AbapCatalog.sqlViewName: 'sql_view_name'
@AbapCatalog.compiler.compareFilter: true
@AbapCatalog.preserveKey: true
@AccessControl.authorizationCheck: #CHECK
@EndUserText.label: 'Interface View for Business Partner'
define view ZI_BUS_PART as select from data_source_name {

}
```

As discussed in the chapter on CDS, change the sql_view_name, data_source_name and add the components.

Final code would be as follows:

```
@AbapCatalog.sqlViewName: 'ZV_BP'
@AbapCatalog.compiler.compareFilter: true
@AbapCatalog.preserveKey: true
@AccessControl.authorizationCheck: #CHECK
@EndUserText.label: 'Interface View for Business Partner'
define view ZI_BUS_PART
  as select from zbus_part
{
  key bpkey,
    partner,
    type,
    bpkind,
    bu_group,
    name_last,
    name_first
}
```

Save and Activate the View.

Create an Interface CDS View (ZBP_IDENTITY) for the BP Identification table and update the placeholders.

The code should be as follows:

```
@AbapCatalog.sqlViewName: 'ZV_BP_ID'
@AbapCatalog.compiler.compareFilter: true
@AbapCatalog.preserveKey: true
@AccessControl.authorizationCheck: #CHECK
@EndUserText.label: 'Business Partner Identification'
define view ZI_BP_IDENTITY
  as select from zbp_identity
{
  key id_key,
    parentkey,
    type,
    idnumber,
    institute,
    cntry_date,
    valid_date_from,
```

```
            valid_date_to,
            country,
            region
    }
```

Save and Activate the View.

1.3 Create the Transactional Processing View

Transactional View are required for Transactional processing. In this step we will create a BOPF object out of the CDS views we created in Section 3.

Create a new data definition file (under core data services) for the Business Partner Root data.

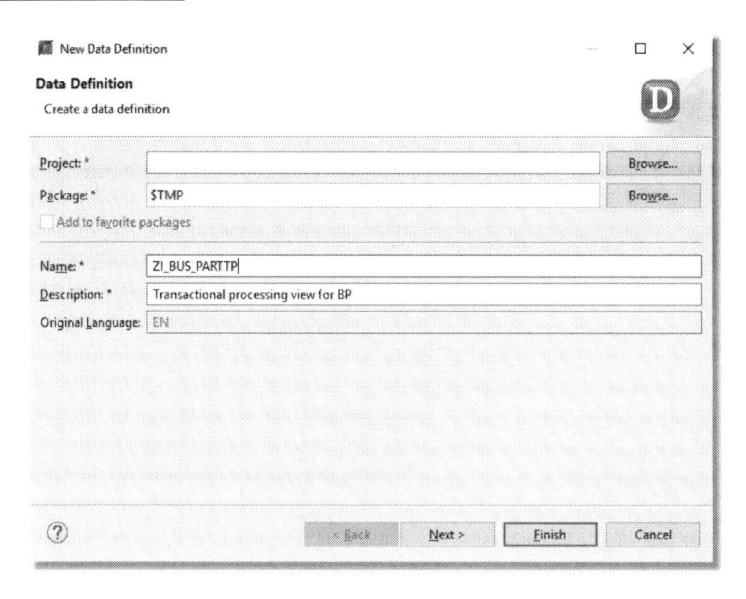

Figure 5: Create BP Interface View

Please note that the name of the View ends with 'TP'. This stands for Transactional processing and helps in identifying the views easily. The general guidance is to use the same name as the Basic view and end with a Suffix 'TP'.

Select the 'Define View' in the Template.

The generate code is as shown below:

```
@AbapCatalog.sqlViewName: 'sql_view_name'
@AbapCatalog.compiler.compareFilter: true
@AbapCatalog.preserveKey: true
@AccessControl.authorizationCheck: #CHECK
@EndUserText.label: 'Transactional processing view for BP'
define view ZI_BUS_PARTTP as select from data_source_name {

}
```

For a transactional view the data source would be the base view created in the previous section

Also, the list of components will the fields exposed by the base view.

The code after making the above changes would be as follows:

```
@AbapCatalog.sqlViewName: 'ZI_BUSPTP'
@AbapCatalog.compiler.compareFilter: true
@AbapCatalog.preserveKey: true
@AccessControl.authorizationCheck: #CHECK
@EndUserText.label: 'Transactional processing view for BP'
define view ZI_BUS_PARTTP
  as select from ZI_BUS_PART
{
  key bpkey,
    partner,
    type,
    bpkind,
    bu_group,
    name_last,
  name_first

}
```

Please note that till now we have just created another view which selects from the base view. To make this view a Transactional processing view which is draft enabled we must add a few more annotations.

- **VDM view type**

@VDM.viewType: #TRANSACTIONAL

- **Object Model Annotations**

    @ObjectModel.transactionalProcessingEnabled: true

    @ObjectModel.compositionRoot: true

    @ObjectModel.writeDraftPersistence: 'ZIBPTPD' - Specify the Draft table

    @ObjectModel.writeActivePersistence:'ZBUS_PARTNER' – Specify the Active table

    @ObjectModel.draftEnabled:true @ObjectModel.createEnabled: true

    @ObjectModel.deleteEnabled: true @ObjectModel.updateEnabled: true

    @ObjectModel.usageType.dataClass: #TRANSACTIONAL

    @ObjectModel.modelCategory: #BUSINESS_OBJECT

The Final code for this Transactional Processing view would be as follows:

```
@AbapCatalog.sqlViewName: 'ZI_BUSPTP'
@AbapCatalog.compiler.compareFilter: true
@AbapCatalog.preserveKey: true

@AccessControl.authorizationCheck: #CHECK

@EndUserText.label: 'Transactional processing view for BP'

@VDM.viewType: #TRANSACTIONAL

@ObjectModel.transactionalProcessingEnabled: true
@ObjectModel.modelCategory: #BUSINESS_OBJECT
@ObjectModel.compositionRoot: true
@ObjectModel.writeDraftPersistence: 'ZIBUSPTPD'
@ObjectModel.writeActivePersistence:'ZBUS_PART'
@ObjectModel.draftEnabled:true
@ObjectModel.createEnabled: true
@ObjectModel.deleteEnabled: true
@ObjectModel.updateEnabled: true
@ObjectModel.usageType.dataClass: #TRANSACTIONAL


define view ZI_BUS_PARTTP
 as select from ZI_BUS_PART
```

```
{
 key bpkey,
    partner,
    type,
    bpkind,
    bu_group,
    name_last,
    name_first

}
```

Save and Activate the View.

The activation of the TP view generates the following 2 objects:

- Draft table for storing the temporary data. This is the table name that was specified as part of the Annotations.

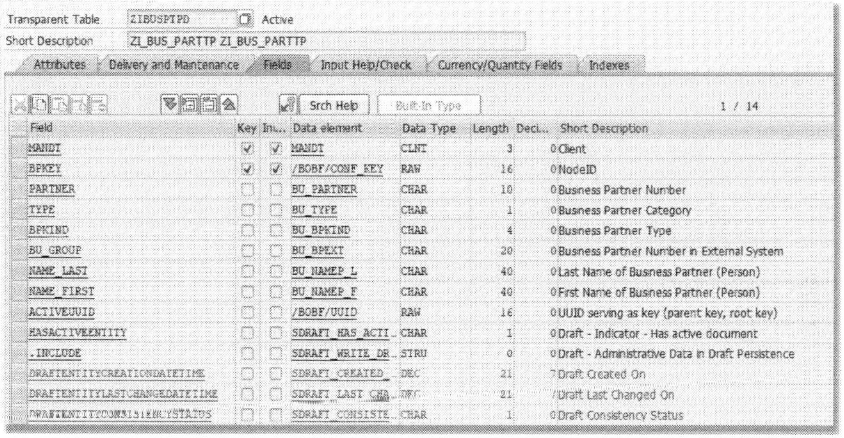

Transparent Table: ZIBUSPTPD Active

Short Description: ZI_BUS_PARTTP ZI_BUS_PARTTP

Attributes | Delivery and Maintenance | Fields | Input Help/Check | Currency/Quantity Fields | Indexes

Srch Help | Built-In Type | 1 / 14

Field	Key	In...	Data element	Data Type	Length	Deci...	Short Description
MANDT	✓	✓	MANDT	CLNT	3	0	Client
BPKEY	✓	✓	/BOBF/CONF_KEY	RAW	16	0	NodeID
PARTNER			BU_PARTNER	CHAR	10	0	Business Partner Number
TYPE			BU_TYPE	CHAR	1	0	Business Partner Category
BPKIND			BU_BPKIND	CHAR	4	0	Business Partner Type
BU_GROUP			BU_BPEXT	CHAR	20	0	Business Partner Number in External System
NAME_LAST			BU_NAMEP_L	CHAR	40	0	Last Name of Business Partner (Person)
NAME_FIRST			BU_NAMEP_F	CHAR	40	0	First Name of Business Partner (Person)
ACTIVEUUID			/BOBF/UUID	RAW	16	0	UUID serving as key (parent key, root key)
HASACTIVEENTITY			SDRAFT_HAS_ACTI...	CHAR	1	0	Draft - Indicator - Has active document
.INCLUDE			SDRAFT_WRITE_DR...	STRU	0	0	Draft - Administrative Data in Draft Persistence
DRAFTENTITYCREATIONDATETIME			SDRAFT_CREATED_...	DEC	21	7	Draft Created On
DRAFTENTITYLASTCHANGEDATETIME			SDRAFT_LAST_CHA...	DEC	21	7	Draft Last Changed On
DRAFTENTITYCONSISTENCYSTATUS			SDRAFT_CONSISTE...	CHAR	1	0	Draft Consistency Status

Figure 6: Display BP Draft table

The system adds 3 fields to store draft related data.

- DRAFTENTITYCREATIONDATETIME – Draft Create On
- DRAFTENTITYLASTCHANGEDATETIME – Draft Last Changed On

- o   DRAFTENTITYCONSISTENCYSTATUS – Draft Consistency Status

- BOPF object for the Business partner with the same as the Transactional processing view.

    This can either be displayed in Eclipse or in the BOBX transaction. (you might have to refresh the View in the Eclipse to see the object)

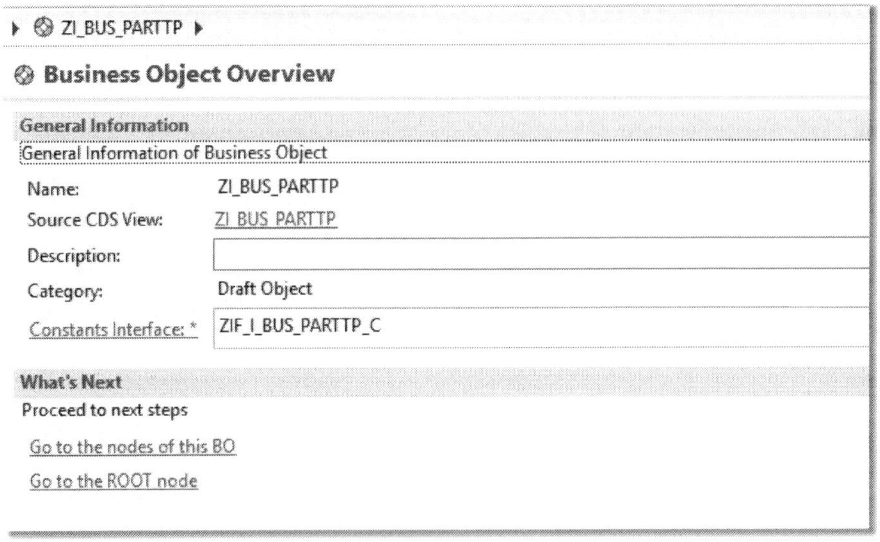

Figure 7: Display Generated BOPF object

This object only has one node as the Identification View does not have any association with the BP General data view.

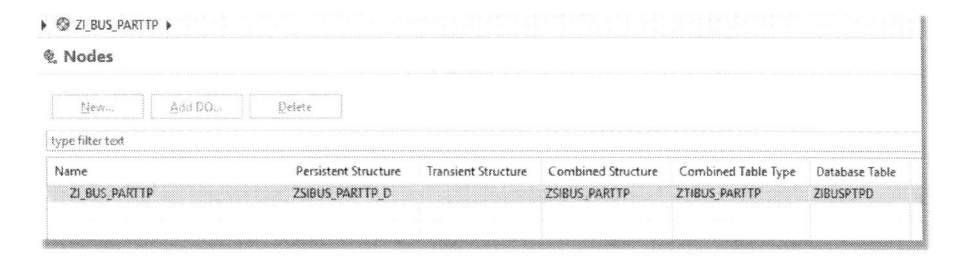

Name	Persistent Structure	Transient Structure	Combined Structure	Combined Table Type	Database Table
ZI_BUS_PARTTP	ZSIBUS_PARTTP_D		ZSIBUS_PARTTP	ZTIBUS_PARTTP	ZIBUSPTPD

Figure 8: Display BOPF nodes of BP object

Create a Transactional Processing view for the Business Partner Identification data.

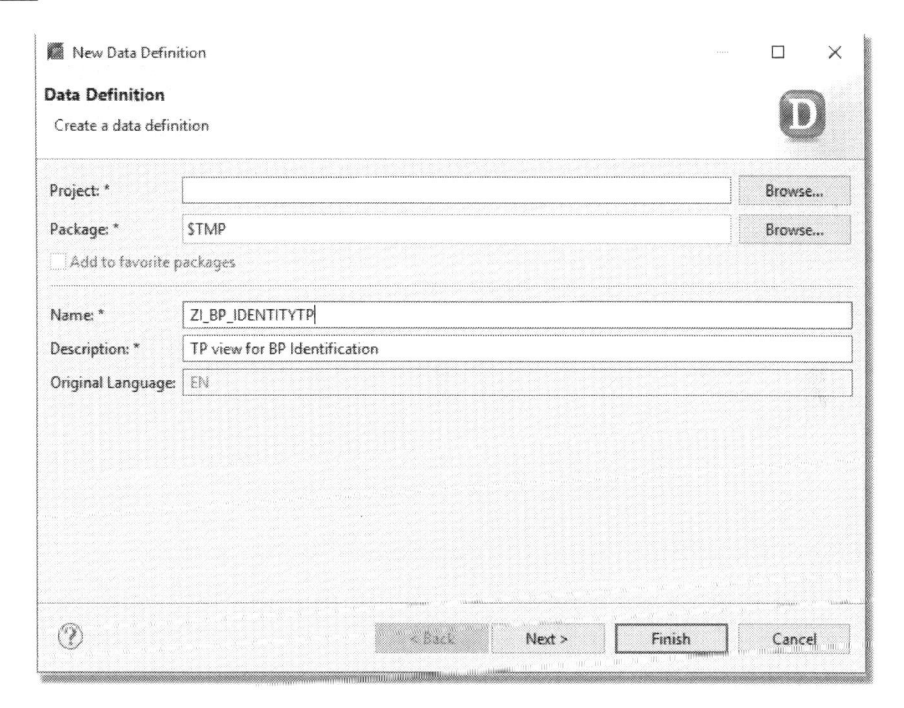

Figure 9: Create Identification Interface View

Change the data source, provide a Sql View name and add the components.

The code at this stage would be as follows:

```
@AbapCatalog.sqlViewName: 'ZV_BP_IDTP'
@AbapCatalog.compiler.compareFilter: true
@AccessControl.authorizationCheck: #CHECK
@EndUserText.label: 'TP view for BP Identification'

define view ZI_BP_IDENTITYTP as select from ZI_BP_IDENTITY {
  key id_key,
    parentkey,
    type,
    idnumber,
    institute,
    entry_date,
    valid_date_from,
    valid_date_to,
    country,
    region
}
```

Like the previous section, this is just another view which reads from the Base CDS view. Now we must add annotations so that the system understands that this view is used for Transactional processing.

Please add the following annotations to this view:

- **VDM view type**

    @VDM.viewType: #TRANSACTIONAL

- **Object Model Annotations**

    @ObjectModel.transactionalProcessingEnabled: true

    @ObjectModel.writeDraftPersistence: ''

    @ObjectModel.writeActivePersistence:'/LOANSWP/DEALI'

    @ObjectModel.createEnabled: true

    @ObjectModel.deleteEnabled: true

    @ObjectModel.updateEnabled: true

    @ObjectModel.usageType.dataClass: #TRANSACTIONAL

Please note that for this view we will not add the below annotations.

    @ObjectModel.compositionRoot: true

@ObjectModel.modelCategory: #BUSINESS_OBJECT

This is because the identification data is a sub node of the BP general data node. The association to the BP TP View would be created in the next section.

Save and Activate the TP View.

The final code after executing the above-mentioned steps is as follows:

```
@AbapCatalog.sqlViewName: 'ZV_BP_IDTP'
@AbapCatalog.compiler.compareFilter: true

@AccessControl.authorizationCheck: #CHECK

@EndUserText.label: 'TP view for BP Identification'

@VDM.viewType: #TRANSACTIONAL
@ObjectModel.transactionalProcessingEnabled: true

@ObjectModel.writeDraftPersistence: 'ZBPIDENTITD'
@ObjectModel.writeActivePersistence:'ZBP_IDENTITY'
@ObjectModel.draftEnabled: true
@ObjectModel.createEnabled: true
@ObjectModel.deleteEnabled: true
@ObjectModel.updateEnabled: true
@ObjectModel.usageType.dataClass: #TRANSACTIONAL

define view ZI_BP_IDENTITYTP
  as select from ZI_BP_IDENTITY
{
  key id_key,
    parentkey,
    type,
    idnumber,
    institute,
    entry_date,
    valid_date_from,
    valid_date_to,
    country,
    region
}
```

On Activation, a Draft table for the Identification data is generated by the system.

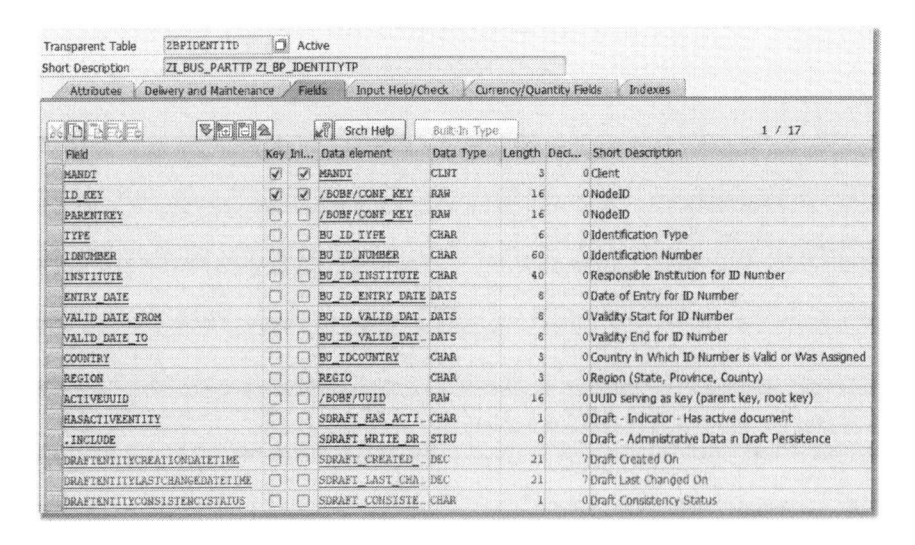

Figure 10: Display Identification Draft table

Create Association between the BP header and the Identification views

In the previous step we have created the Basic views and the Transactional processing views. But these views are independent. In this Step we will create an association between the views so that the Identification data is created as a Sub-node of the BP data. This will also regenerate the BOPF object.

To Create an association, add the below highlighted code in the TP views:

- **ZI_BUS_PARTTP**:

    @AbapCatalog.sqlViewName: 'ZI_BUSPTP'
    @AbapCatalog.compiler.compareFilter: true
    @AbapCatalog.preserveKey: true

    @AccessControl.authorizationCheck: #CHECK

    @EndUserText.label: 'Transactional processing view for BP'

    @VDM.viewType: #TRANSACTIONAL

```
@ObjectModel.transactionalProcessingEnabled: true
@ObjectModel.modelCategory: #BUSINESS_OBJECT
@ObjectModel.compositionRoot: true
@ObjectModel.writeDraftPersistence: 'ZIBUSPTPD'
@ObjectModel.writeActivePersistence:'ZBUS_PART'
@ObjectModel.draftEnabled:true
@ObjectModel.createEnabled: true
@ObjectModel.deleteEnabled: true
@ObjectModel.updateEnabled: true
@ObjectModel.usageType.dataClass: #TRANSACTIONAL

define view ZI_BUS_PARTTP
  as select from ZI_BUS_PART
  association [1..*] to ZI_BP_IDENTITYTP as _BPIdent on $projection.bpkey = _BPIdent.parentkey
{
  key bpkey,
    partner,
    type,
    bpkind,
    bu_group,
    name_last,
    name_first,

    @ObjectModel.association.type: [#TO_COMPOSITION_CHILD]
    _BPIdent

}
```

- **ZI_BP_IDENTITYTP:**

    @AbapCatalog.sqlViewName: 'ZV_BP_IDTP'
    @AbapCatalog.compiler.compareFilter: true

    @AccessControl.authorizationCheck: #CHECK

    @EndUserText.label: 'TP view for BP Identification'

    @VDM.viewType: #TRANSACTIONAL
    @ObjectModel.transactionalProcessingEnabled: true

    @ObjectModel.writeDraftPersistence: 'ZBPIDENTITD'
    @ObjectModel.writeActivePersistence:'ZBP_IDENTITY'
    @ObjectModel.draftEnabled: true
    @ObjectModel.createEnabled: true
    @ObjectModel.deleteEnabled: true

@ObjectModel.updateEnabled: true
@ObjectModel.usageType.dataClass: #TRANSACTIONAL

define view ZI_BP_IDENTITYTP
  as select from zi_bp_identity
  association [1..1] to ZI_BUS_PARTTP as _BPHeader on $projection.parentkey = _BPHeader.bpkey
{
  key id_key,
     parentkey,
     type,
     idnumber,
     institute,
     entry_date,
     valid_date_from,
     valid_date_to,
     country,
     region,
     @ObjectModel.association.type: [#TO_COMPOSITION_ROOT,#TO_COMPOSITION_PARENT]
     _BPHeader

}

Now Activate both the TP views together.

After activation the BOPF object is regenerated. The object now has a Sub-node for Identification data.

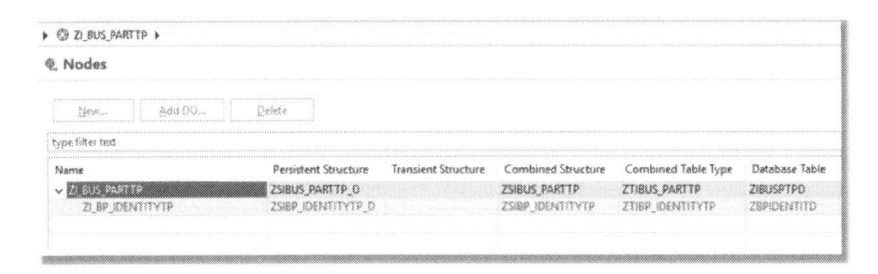

Figure 11: Display Nodes of BP BOPF object

<u>Execute the BOPF object and test the Draft functionality.</u>

As explained in the beginning of this chapter, whenever the focus on the field changes on the screen the temporary data is saved in the Draft table. This helps in recovery of data in case of Crash or if the Brower was closed by mistake.

On Save of the data, the entry from the Draft table is copied to the Active data (The UUIDs are of course different). After the data is copied, the data from the Draft table is deleted.

- Check the data of the Draft and Active Partner table. This should be empty as no data has been created

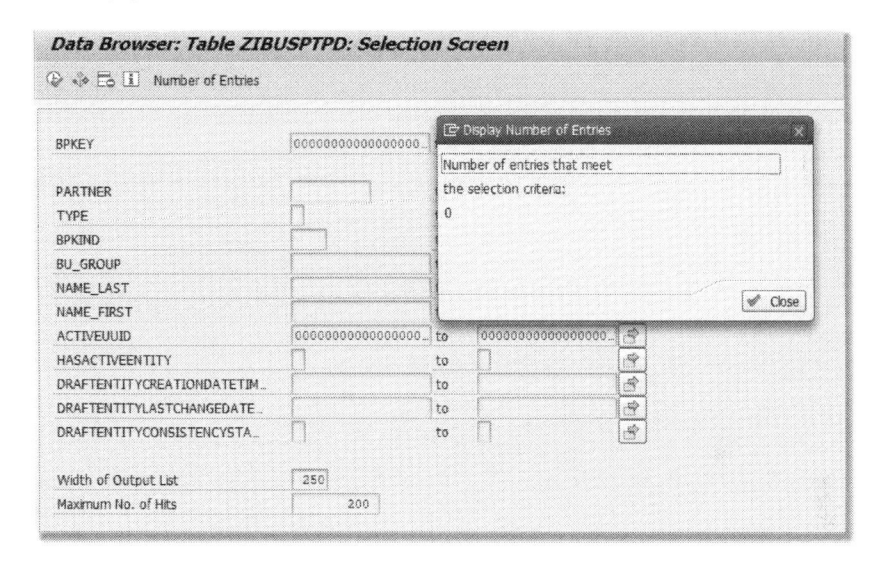

Figure 12: Display entires in Draft table

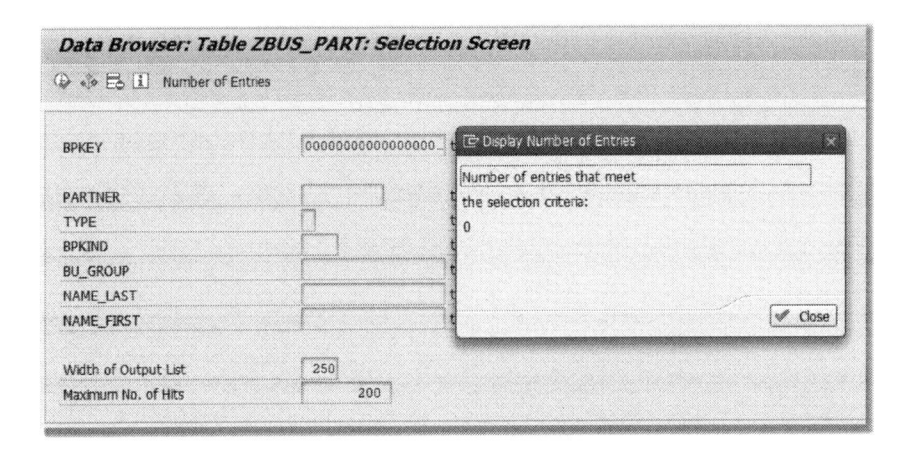

Figure 13: Display entries in BP Active table

- Execute the BOBT transaction and Create a new entry for the partner data
  Click on the Create New Entry button.

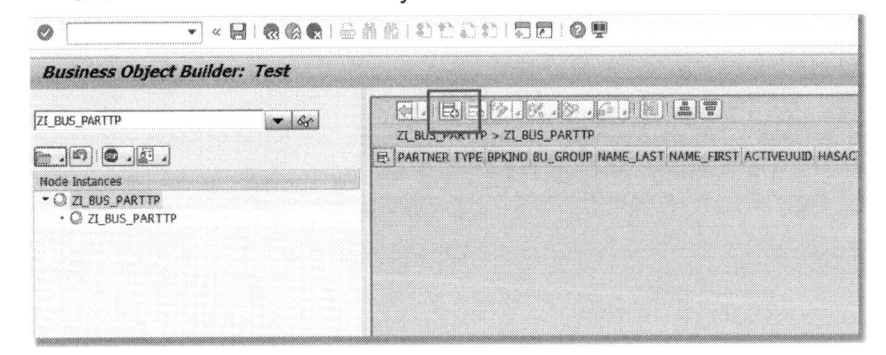

Figure 14: Create new BP

Enter the Partner details

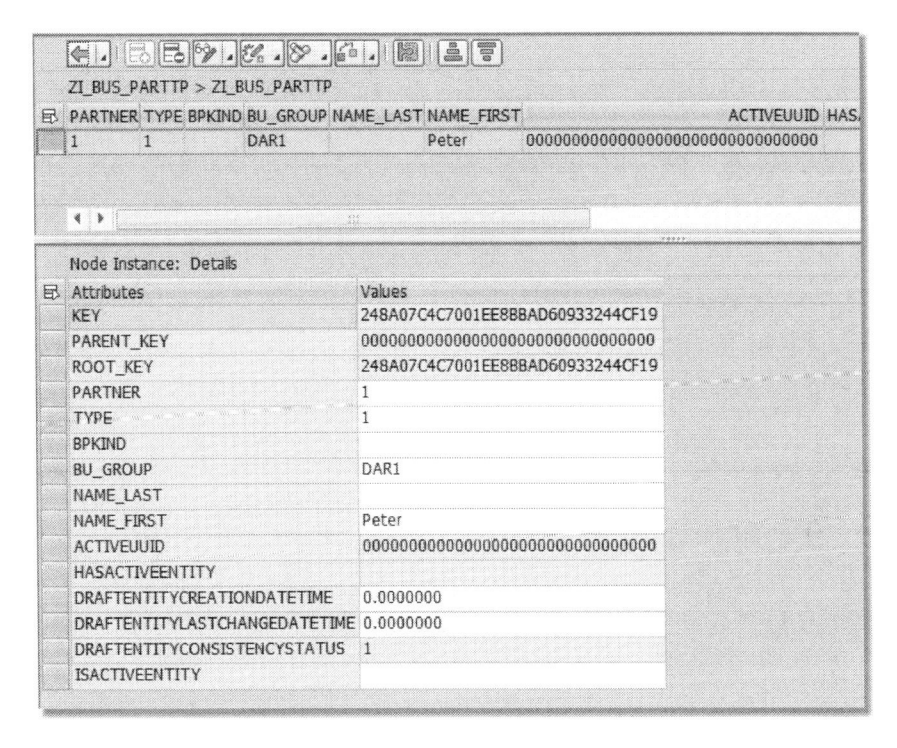

Figure 15: Enter BP General data

To Enter the details of the Identification for the BP data entered, Select the BP data and click on 'Execute Association'.

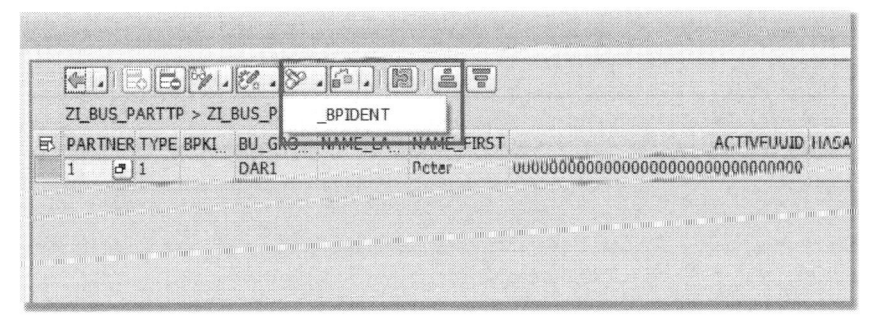

Figure 16: Execute Identification Assiciation

Enter the details of the identification:

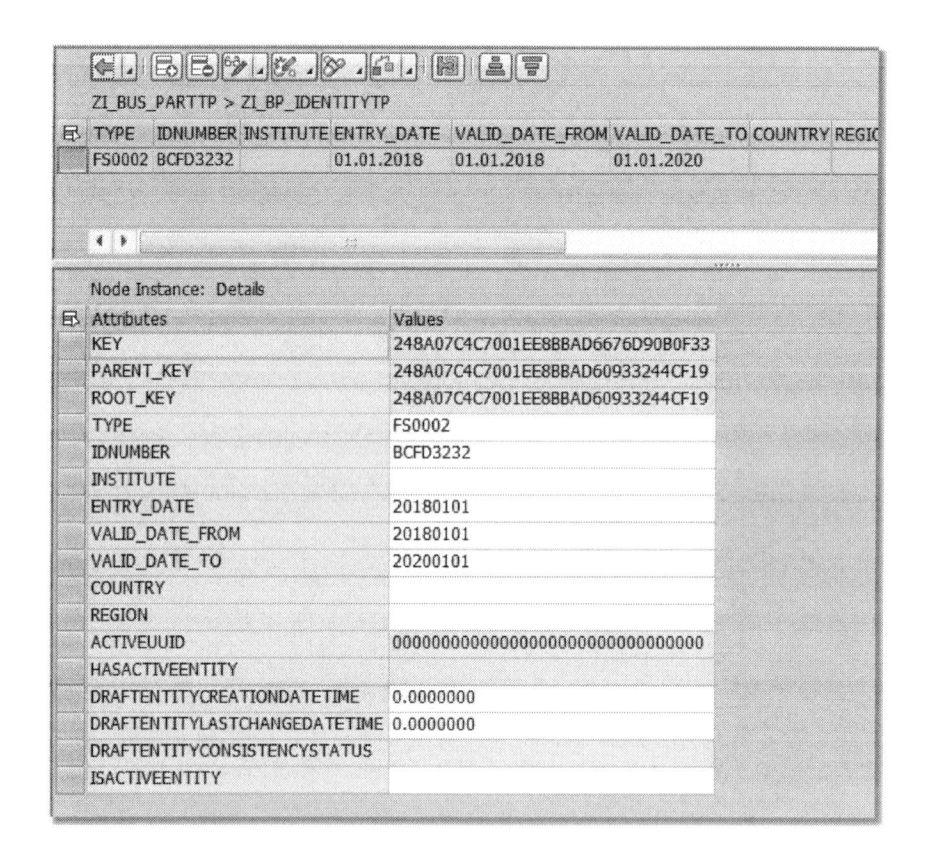

Figure 17: Enter Identification data

After entering the data click on Save. The system now stores the data in the Draft table.

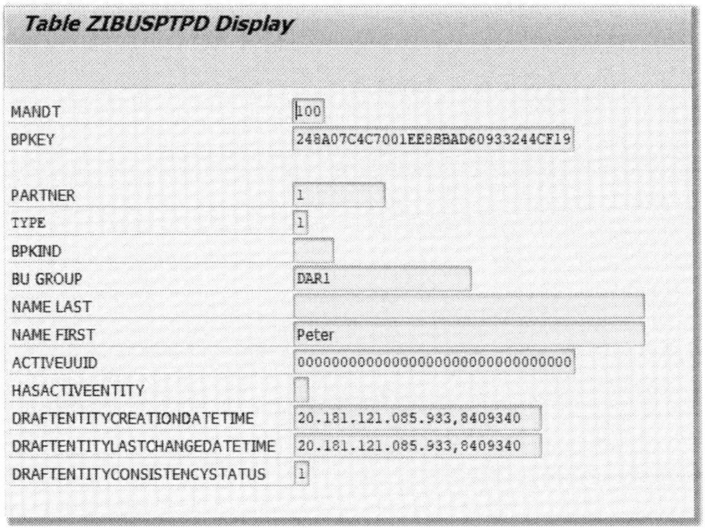

Table ZIBUSPTPD Display

MANDT	100
BPKEY	248A07C4C7001EE8BBAD60933244CF19
PARTNER	1
TYPE	1
BPKIND	
BU GROUP	DAR1
NAME LAST	
NAME FIRST	Peter
ACTIVEUUID	00000000000000000000000000000000
HASACTIVEENTITY	
DRAFTENTITYCREATIONDATETIME	20.181.121.085.933,8409340
DRAFTENTITYLASTCHANGEDATETIME	20.181.121.085.933,8409340
DRAFTENTITYCONSISTENCYSTATUS	1

Figure 18: Check BP data in Draft table

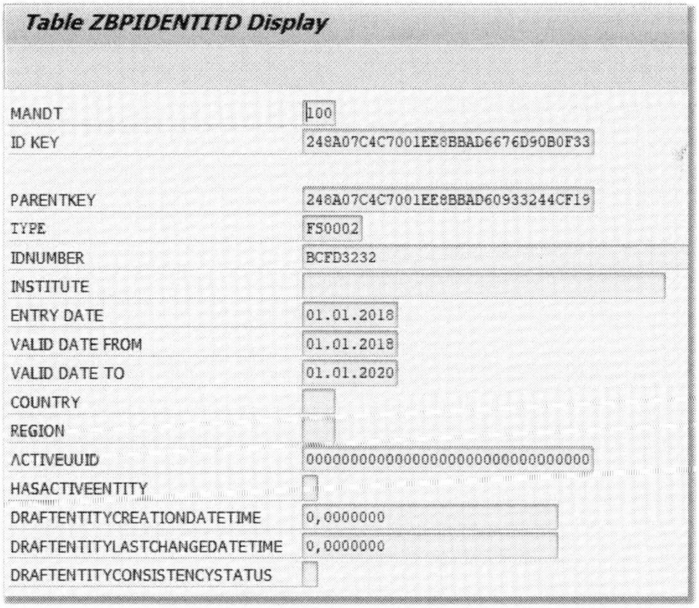

Table ZBPIDENTITD Display

MANDT	100
ID KEY	248A07C4C7001EE8BBAD6676D90B0F33
PARENTKEY	248A07C4C7001EE8BBAD60933244CF19
TYPE	FS0002
IDNUMBER	BCFD3232
INSTITUTE	
ENTRY DATE	01.01.2018
VALID DATE FROM	01.01.2018
VALID DATE TO	01.01.2020
COUNTRY	
REGION	
ACTIVEUUID	00000000000000000000000000000000
HASACTIVEENTITY	
DRAFTENTITYCREATIONDATETIME	0,0000000
DRAFTENTITYLASTCHANGEDATETIME	0,0000000
DRAFTENTITYCONSISTENCYSTATUS	

Figure 19: Check BP Identification data in Draft table

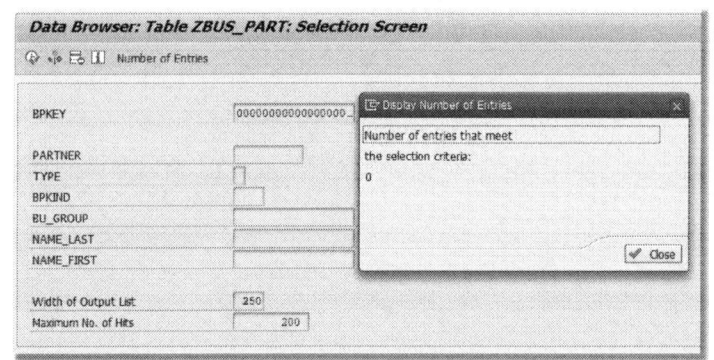

The Active table still does not have any data.

Figure 20: Display Entries in Active BP table

- Let us now Execute the Save Action so that the data is copied from the Draft to the Active table and the data in the Draft table entry is deleted. For this, we must execute 3 steps:

    o Preparation
    o Validation
    o Activation

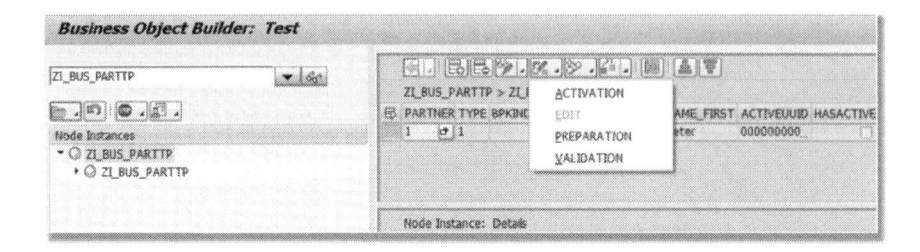

Figure 21: Execute Actions on Data

The steps should be executed in the same order as mentioned.
Once done, Click on Save.

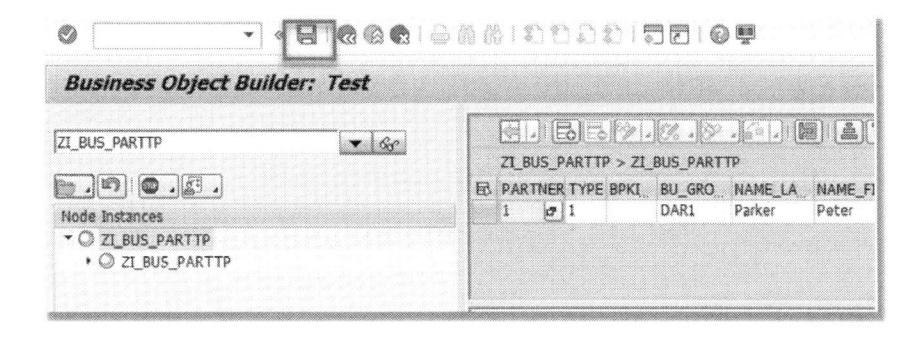

Figure 22: Save BP data to Active table

Now check the data in the Draft and Active tables. The data in the Draft table has been deleted and the data has been copied to the Active table. The new UUIDs of the Active table were of course generated.

Figure 23: Display BP data in Active table

Figure 24: Display Identification data in Active table

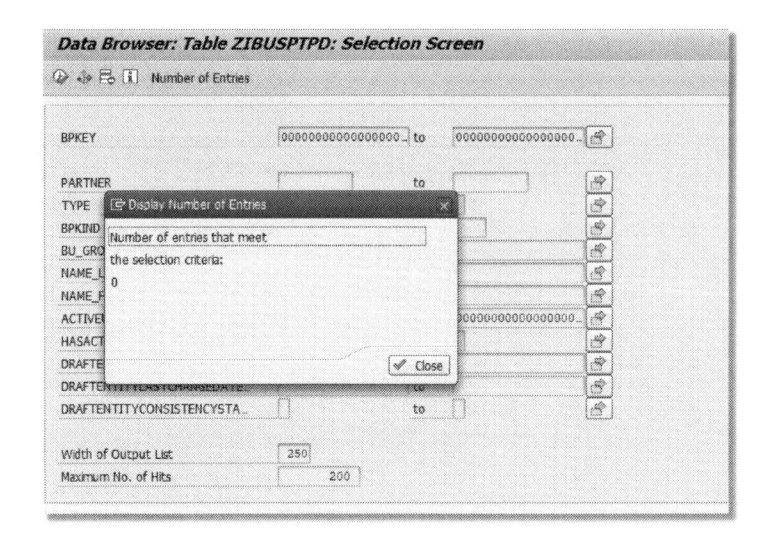

Figure 25: Display data in Draft table

1.4 Create the Consumption View for the User Interface

Create a new data definition file (under core data services) as shown

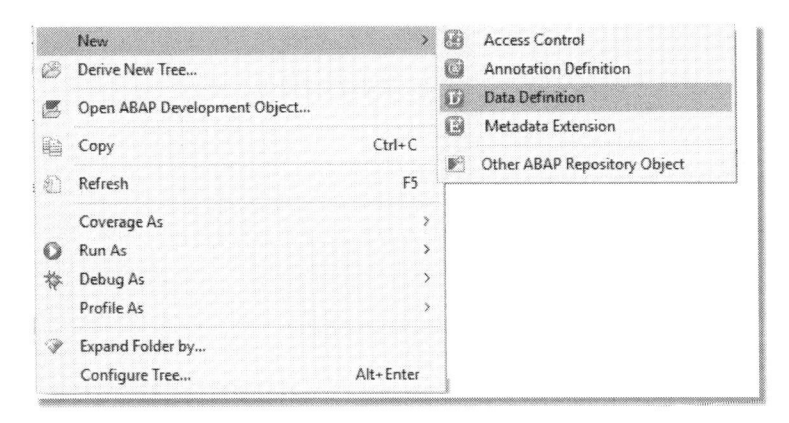

Figure 26: Create BP Consumption View

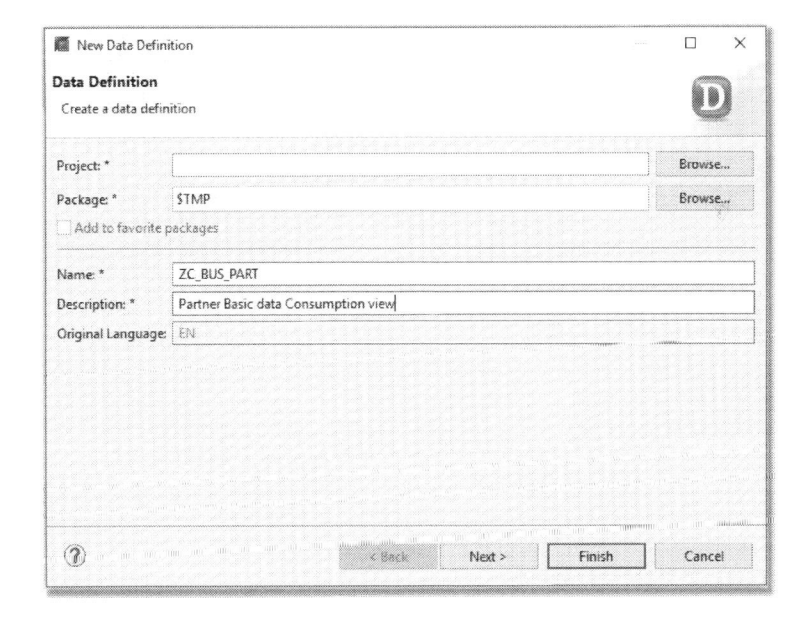

Figure 27: Create BP Consumption View

Like the previous steps, replace the SQL View, data source and add the components.

Here the consumption view would select from the Transactional processing view.

Add the following Annotations for the consumption view

```
@Metadata.allowExtensions: true
@VDM.viewType: #CONSUMPTION
@ObjectModel.createEnabled: true
@ObjectModel.updateEnabled: true
@ObjectModel.deleteEnabled: true
@ObjectModel.draftEnabled: true
@ObjectModel.compositionRoot: true
@ObjectModel.transactionalProcessingDelegated: true
```

The code of the consumption view would be as follows:

```
@AbapCatalog.sqlViewName: 'ZC_BUSPTP'
@AbapCatalog.compiler.compareFilter: true
@AbapCatalog.preserveKey: true
@AccessControl.authorizationCheck: #CHECK
@EndUserText.label: 'Partner Basic data Consumption view'

@Metadata.allowExtensions: true
@VDM.viewType: #CONSUMPTION
@ObjectModel.createEnabled: true
@ObjectModel.updateEnabled: true
@ObjectModel.deleteEnabled: true
@ObjectModel.draftEnabled: true
@ObjectModel.compositionRoot: true
@ObjectModel.transactionalProcessingDelegated: true

define view ZC_BUS_PART as select from ZI_BUS_PARTTP {

    key bpkey,
        partner,
        type,
        bpkind,
        bu_group,
        name_last,
        name_first

}
```

Like the Consumption view of Business Partner General data, create a consumption view for the BP Identification data.

The code of the BP Identification Consumption View would be as follows:

```
@AbapCatalog.sqlViewName: 'ZC_BP_IDTP'
@AbapCatalog.compiler.compareFilter: true
@AbapCatalog.preserveKey: true
@AccessControl.authorizationCheck: #CHECK
@EndUserText.label: 'BP Identification data Consumption View'

@Metadata.allowExtensions: true
@VDM.viewType: #CONSUMPTION
@ObjectModel.createEnabled: true
@ObjectModel.updateEnabled: true
@ObjectModel.deleteEnabled: true
@ObjectModel.draftEnabled: true
@ObjectModel.compositionRoot: true
@ObjectModel.transactionalProcessingDelegated: true

define view ZC_BP_IDENTITY as select from ZI_BP_IDENTITYTP {

    key id_key,
    parentkey,
    type,
    idnumber,
    institute,
    entry_date,
    valid_date_from,
    valid_date_to,
    country,
    region
}
```

Add the association between the BP General data and Identification Consumption views

This is same as it was done for the Transactional Processing views.

The code after this step would be as follows:

```
@AbapCatalog.sqlViewName: 'ZC_BUSPTP'
@AbapCatalog.compiler.compareFilter: true
@AbapCatalog.preserveKey: true
```

@AccessControl.authorizationCheck: #CHECK
@EndUserText.label: 'Partner Basic data Consumption view'

@Metadata.allowExtensions: true
@VDM.viewType: #CONSUMPTION
@ObjectModel.createEnabled: true
@ObjectModel.updateEnabled: true
@ObjectModel.deleteEnabled: true
@ObjectModel.draftEnabled: true
@ObjectModel.compositionRoot: true
@ObjectModel.transactionalProcessingDelegated: true

define view ZC_BUS_PART
 as select from ZI_BUS_PARTTP
 association [1..*] **to** ZC_BP_IDENTITY **as** _BPIdent **on** $projection.bpkey = _BPIdent.parentkey
{

  key bpkey,
    partner,
    type,
    bpkind,
    bu_group,
    name_last,
    name_first,

    @ObjectModel.association.type: [#TO_COMPOSITION_CHILD]
    _BPIdent
}

@AbapCatalog.sqlViewName: 'ZC_BP_IDTP'
@AbapCatalog.compiler.compareFilter: true
@AbapCatalog.preserveKey: true
@AccessControl.authorizationCheck: #CHECK
@EndUserText.label: 'BP Identification data Consumption View'

@Metadata.allowExtensions: true
@VDM.viewType: #CONSUMPTION
@ObjectModel.createEnabled: true
@ObjectModel.updateEnabled: true
@ObjectModel.deleteEnabled: true
@ObjectModel.draftEnabled: true
@ObjectModel.compositionRoot: true
@ObjectModel.transactionalProcessingDelegated: true

define view ZC_BP_IDENTITY

```
  as select from ZI_BP_IDENTITYTP
   association [1..1] to ZC_BUS_PART as _BPHeader on
  $projection.parentkey = _BPHeader.bpkey
  {

    key id_key,
       parentkey,
       type,
       idnumber,
       institute,
       entry_date,
       valid_date_from,
       valid_date_to,
       country,
       region,

       @ObjectModel.association.type:
  [#TO_COMPOSITION_ROOT,#TO_COMPOSITION_PARENT]
       _BPHeader
  }
```

1.5 Create OData service

In the previous steps we create the Transactional View for CRUD operations and Consumption view for displaying the data in the UI. But the Views can only be consumed form outside world via oData service.

In this step we will generate the oData service for the views so that we can Create and Display the data from UI5.

There are multiple ways to create OData service from CDS Views. Here, we will cover 2 ways. But you would be required to follow only one of the approaches mentioned below.

a) Odata via CDS views Annotation
b) Referenced Data source

The preferred approach is to use 'Referenced Data source' but the approach via CDS Annotation is easy and works well for small projects / POCs.

1.5.1 Generate the oData service from CDS view

Add Annotation @OData.publish: true in both the Consumption Views and Activate it.

You would notice that there is a warning saying the OData service is not activated.

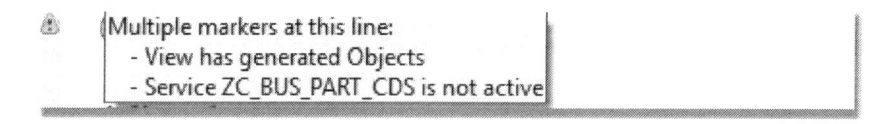

Figure 28: Display marker for OData object

Activate the OData Service:

Execute Transaction '/IWFND/MAINT_SERVICE' in SAP GUI.

Add a service by clicking on 'Add Service'.

Figure 29: Add new BP Service

Check the Co-deployed checkbox and search for your service.

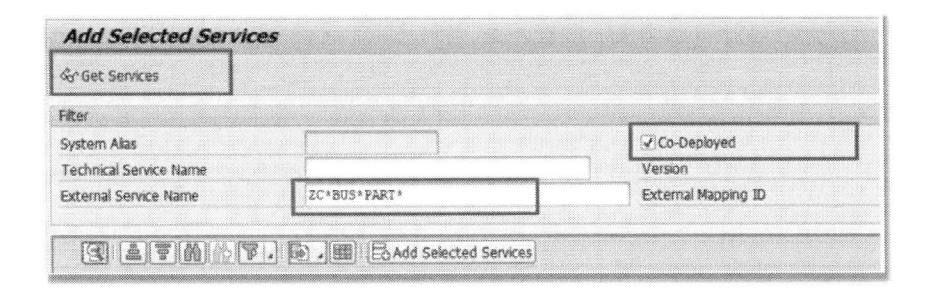

Figure 30: Search for new Service

Select your service and press Add Service.

Figure 31: Add Selected service

To test the service, Select the service and go the SAP Gateway Client.

Select the URI option as '$metadata' and check the service.

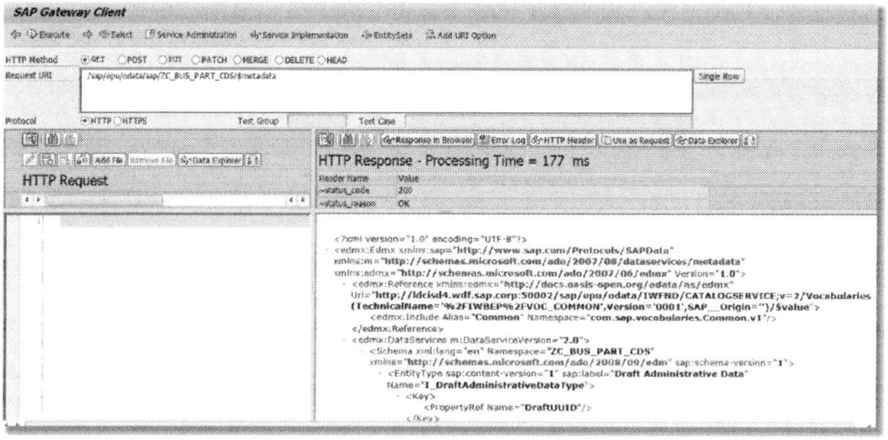

Figure 32: Get the Meta data of the service

Now let us try to retrieve the data which was created. We had created an entry for the BP General data and saved it in the active table via BOPF transaction. It should now be possible to retrieve the data.

In the client enter the Request URI as below:

/sap/opu/odata/sap/ZC_BUS_PART_CDS/ZC_BUS_PART(bpkey=guid'047D7B8B-FE3F-1ED8-B983-B6600DBE4A2B',IsActiveEntity=true)

Please note that you will have to replace the 'bpkey' value with the value of the GUID in your table.

Execute the Request.

The data in the table is returned as shown below:

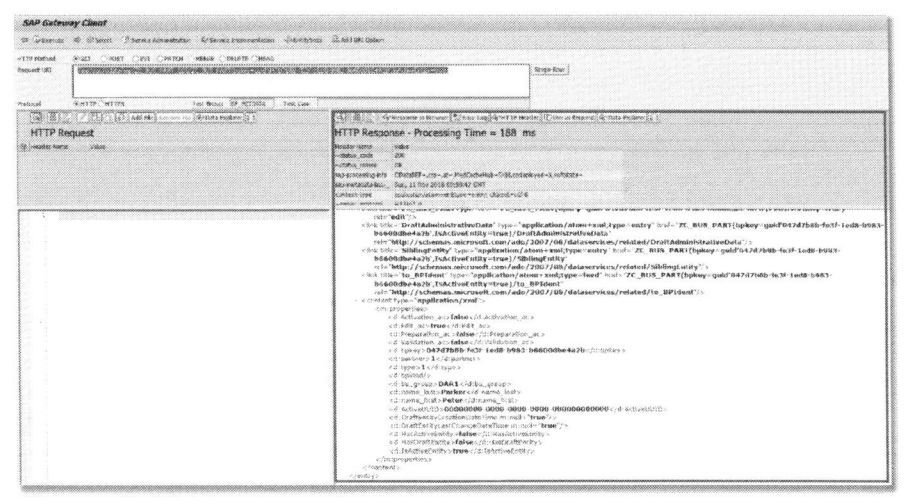

Figure 33: Get the BP data from the Active table

1.5.2 Generate the OData service from CDS view

Click on Create Project and provide the necessary details on Create Project dialog box.

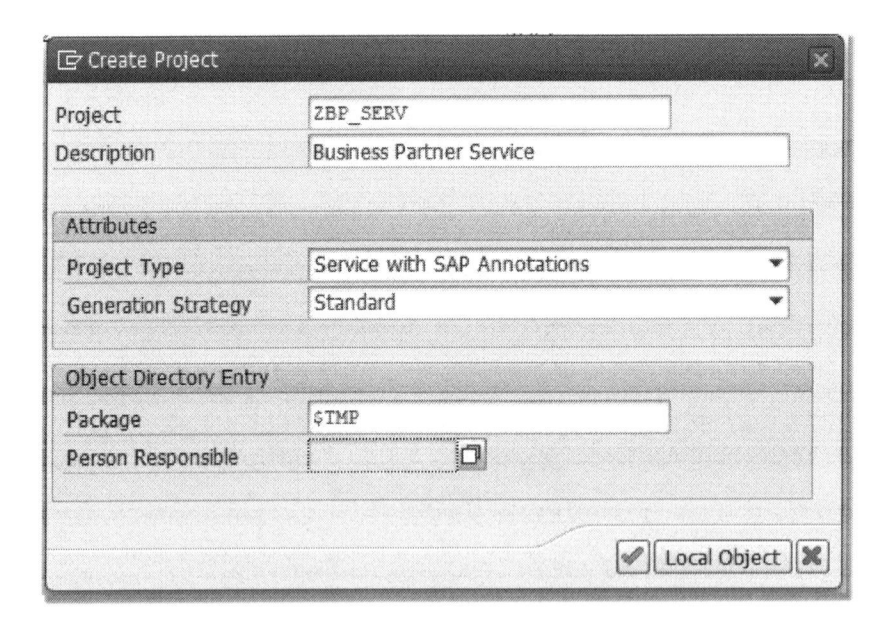

Figure 34: Create New OData project

A new SEGW project will be created with empty data model like below.

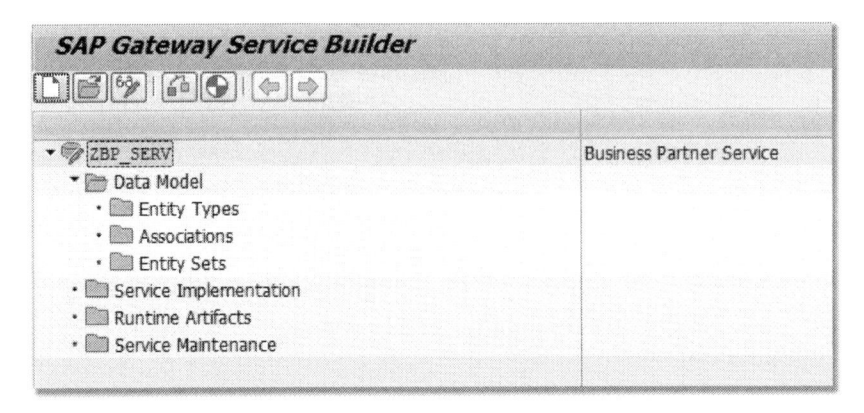

Figure 35: Display OData Project structure

Now right-click on the Data Model choose Reference and then Data Source.

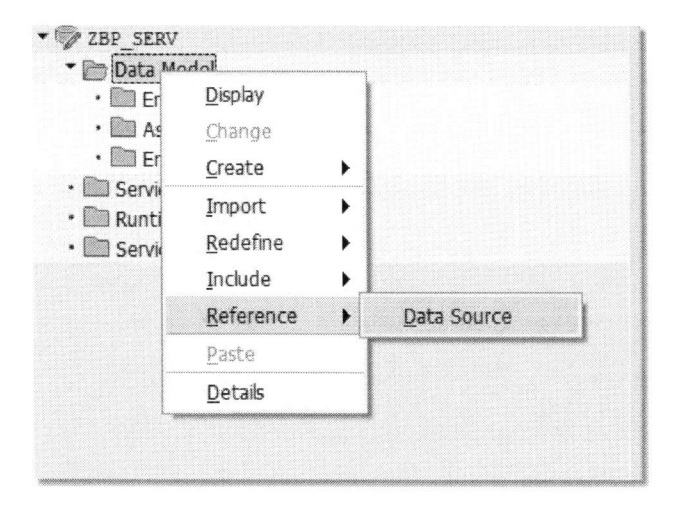

Figure 36: Create Data Model using Referenced Data Sources

A new Reference Data Source wizard will open like below. Choose ABAP CDS view using the F4 help and hit Next.

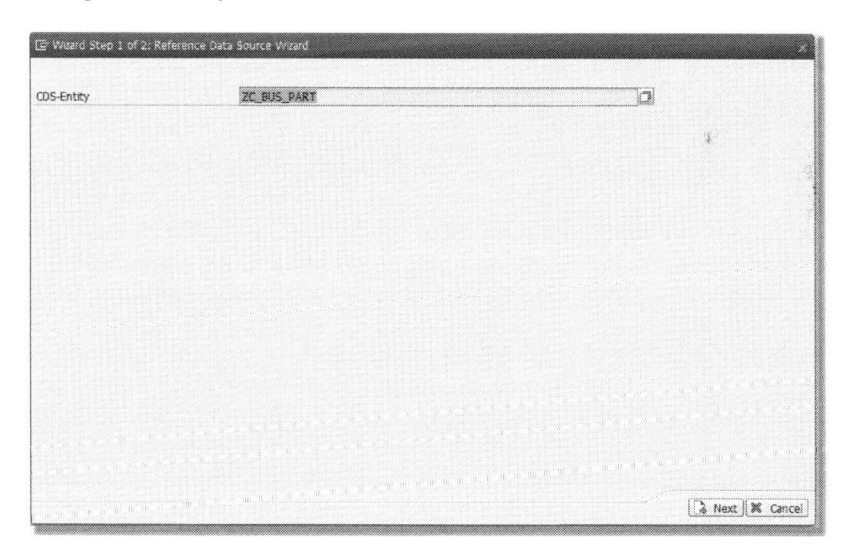

Figure 37: Enter Referenced Data Source

In the next wizard step check the information and hit Finish.

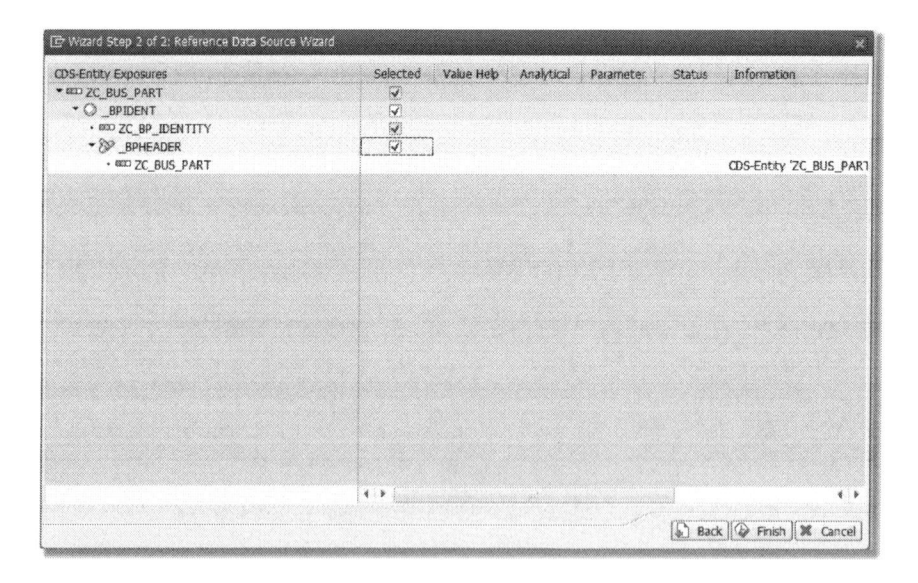

Figure 38: Select the CDS Entity Exposures

ABAP CDS entity will be successfully referenced in the SEGW project and new folder Data Source References will be created under Data Model folder.

```
▼ 🗐 ZBP_SERV                                           Business Partner Service
   ▼ 📂 Data Model
      · 🗀 Entity Types
      · 🗀 Associations
      · 🗀 Entity Sets
   ▼ 📂 Data Source References
      ▼ 📂 Exposures via SADL
         ▼ 🗐 CDS-Entity Exposures
            ▼ 📂 Entity Types
               ▶ ▭ I_DraftAdministrativeDataType
               ▶ ▭ ZC_BP_IDENTITYType
               ▶ ▭ ZC_BUS_PARTType
            ▶ 🗀 Complex Types
            ▼ 📂 Associations
               ▶ 🔗 assoc_172C01B3C52230E254AA20DB09E2ED   ZC_BP_IDENTITY~_DraftAdministrativeDa
               ▶ 🔗 assoc_8EE86D8C871DB68CAA91EE80ADA44E   ZC_BP_IDENTITY~_SiblingEntity
               ▶ 🔗 assoc_916B8EDDF4DE35DE30AC968412A47E   ZC_BUS_PART~_SiblingEntity
               ▶ 🔗 assoc_A926C059EEB8440E3055DD84F81E5A   ZC_BUS_PART~_BPIdent
               ▶ 🔗 assoc_D44EC3080AACF066F584BCFD0E7307I  ZC_BUS_PART~_DraftAdministrativeData
            ▼ 📂 Entity Sets
               · ▭ I_DraftAdministrativeData
               · ▭ ZC_BP_IDENTITY
               · ▭ ZC_BUS_PART
            ▼ 📂 Association Sets
               · 🔗 assoc_172C01B3C52230E254AA20DB09E2ED
               · 🔗 assoc_8EE86D8C871DB68CAA91EE80ADA44E
               · 🔗 assoc_916B8EDDF4DE35DE30AC968412A47E
               · 🔗 assoc_A926C059EEB8440E3055DD84F81E5A
               · 🔗 assoc_D44EC3080AACF066F584BCFD0E7307I
            ▼ 📂 Function Imports
               ▶ ▭ ZC_BP_IDENTITYPreparation
               ▶ ▭ ZC_BP_IDENTITYValidation
               ▶ ▭ ZC_BUS_PARTActivation
               ▶ ▭ ZC_BUS_PARTEdit
               ▶ ▭ ZC_BUS_PARTPreparation
               ▶ ▭ ZC_BUS_PARTValidation
```

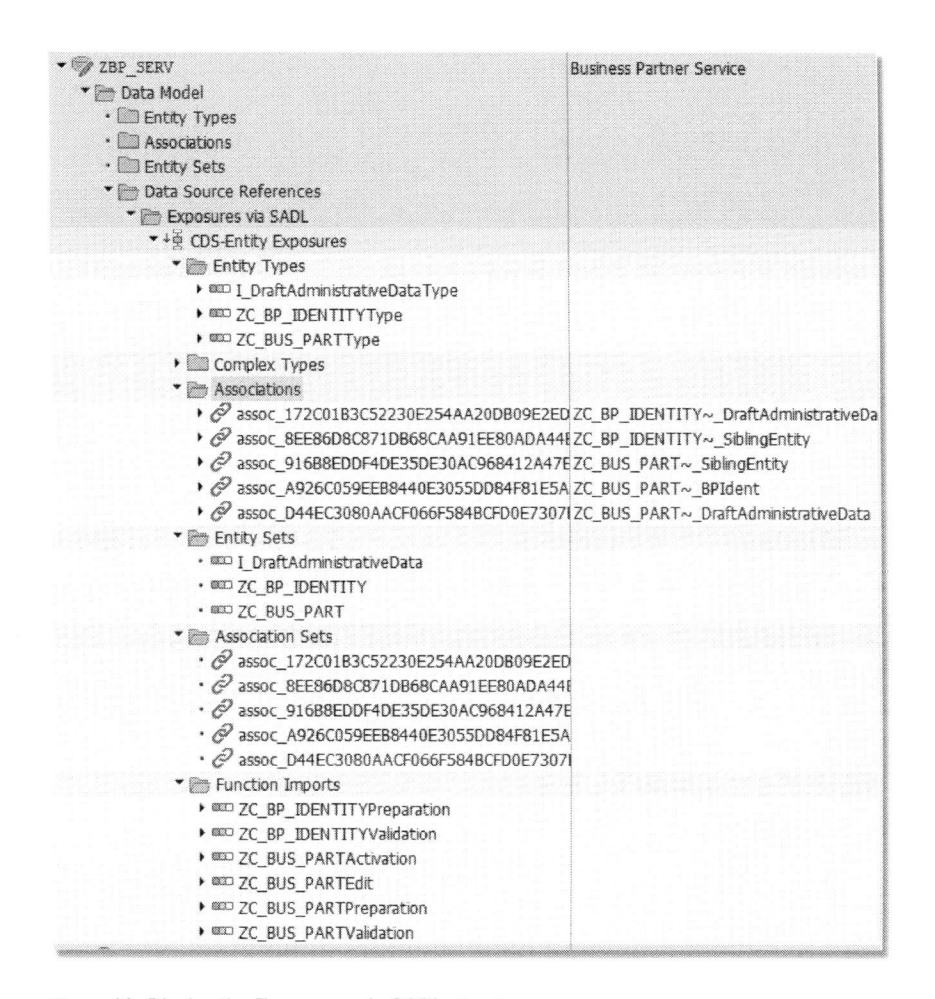

Figure 39: Display the Exposures via SADL structure

Now activate the service. Activation steps are same as what we discussed when we created the service via Annotation.

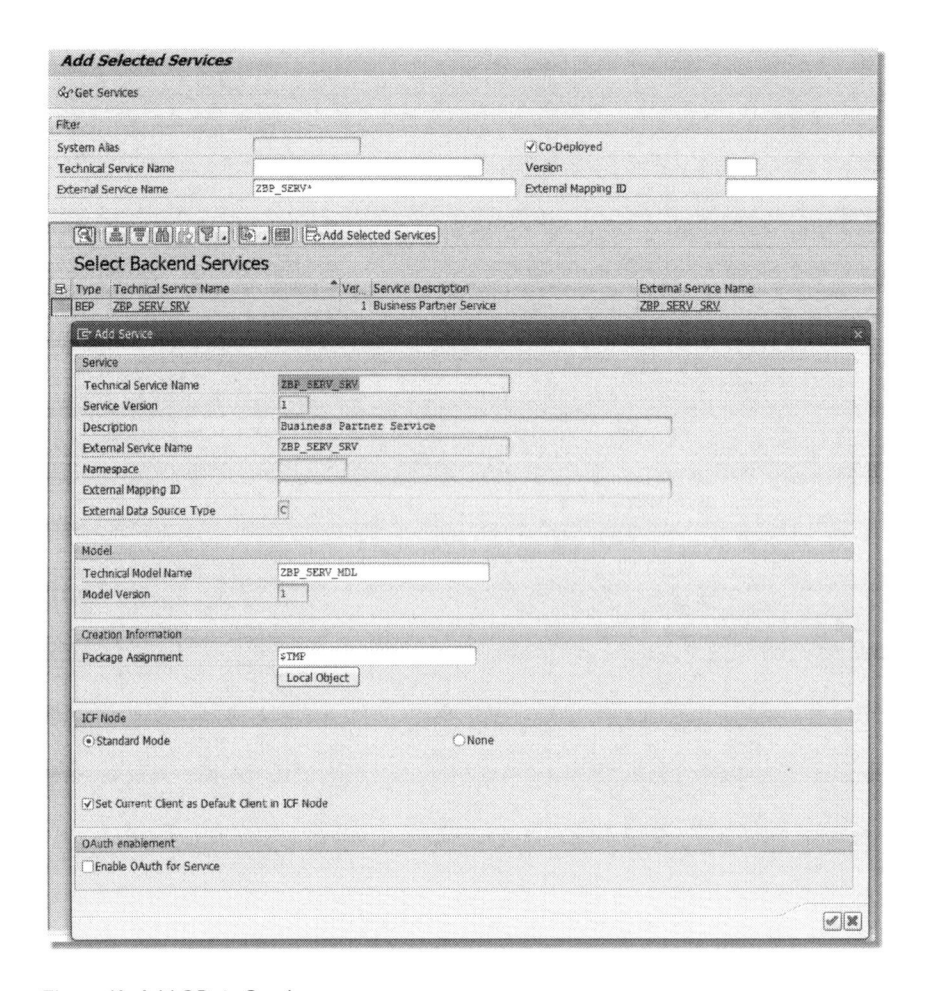

Figure 40: Add OData Service

Now test the service using the below URI:

/sap/opu/odata/sap/ZBP_SERV_SRV/ZC_BUS_PART(bpkey=guid'248A07C4-C700-1EE8-BBAD-95A48E0BCFDA',IsActiveEntity=true)

Do not forget to replace the GUID with your own GUID.

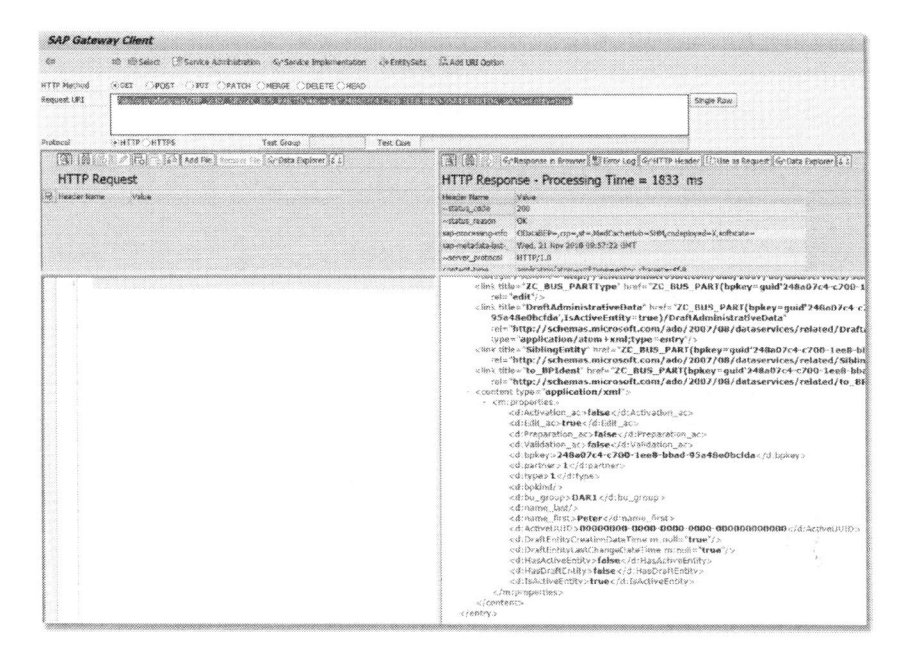

Figure 41: Execute OData Get service

As you can see from above, the data is retrieved and displayed.

1.6 Transactional Processing

In the previous steps we have created all the backend building blocks required to have the application running (Expect UI, as this is not the focus of this book). But we are yet to add business logic.

We will now extend this application by adding various business logic.

Following are some examples of common requirements you might come across in you project work

- Create a Default Identification data in the Identification table as soon as the BP basic data is entered.
  This can be achieved by creating a Determination

- Validate that correct value of Business Partner Group is entered when creating the BP.
  This can be done through a Validation

- Check the data before saving it to the database. To achieve this, we would add an action to check the data before we save it to the active table.

For this exercise we will only implement a Determination and show the necessary steps. The steps to create Validations, Actions remain the same and should be explored.

1.6.1 Add a Determination

To add a determination, open the BOPF object created in Hana Studio and click on 'Go to ROOT node'

Now click on Determinations link to navigate to the list of Determinations.

Click on "New.." to add a new Determination

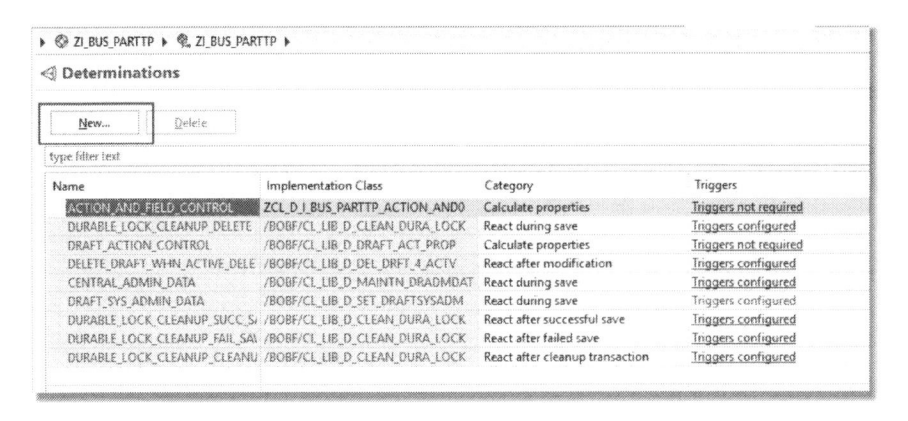

Figure 42: Create New Determination

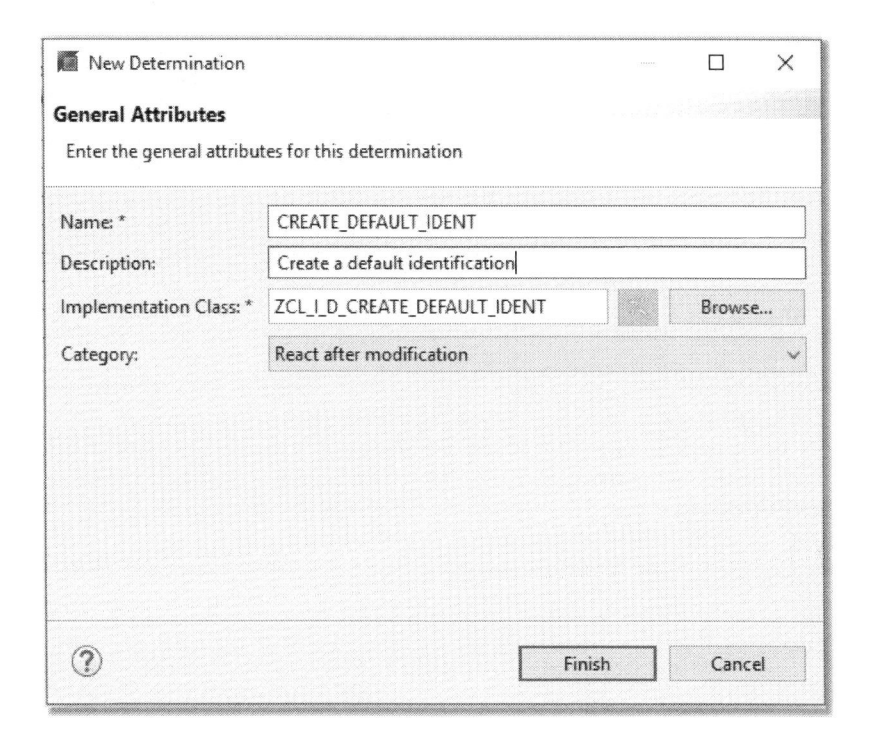

Figure 43: Enter Attributes of New Determination

As you would have noticed, the system automatically proposes the name of the class based on the name of the Determination. Click Finish and activate the Object.

Once done, you would notice that the proposed class is already created with no code.

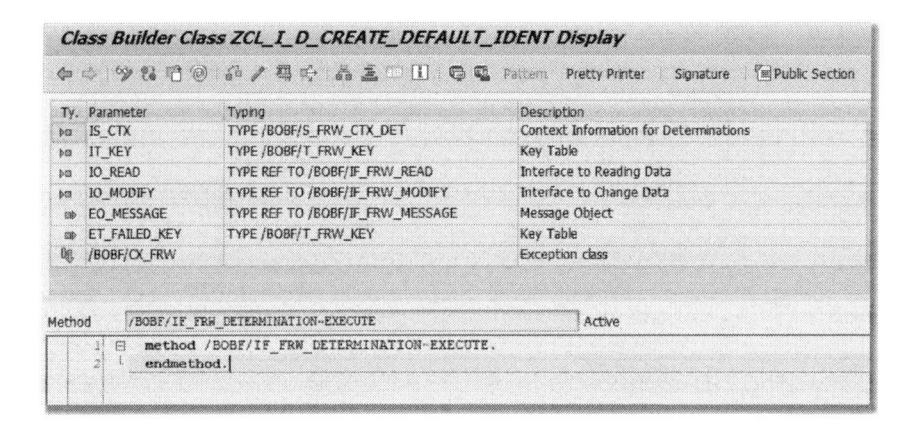

Figure 44: Display Determination class

Now add code to create a default identification data.

METHOD /bobf/if_frw_determination~execute.

DATA: bpidentifications TYPE ztibp_identitytp,
      bp_ident_create   TYPE zsibp_identitytp.

" Get the Draft keys of the BP Generic daa
/bobf/cl_lib_draft=>/bobf/if_lib_union_utilities~separate_keys(
  EXPORTING
   iv_bo_key   = is_ctx-bo_key
   iv_node_key = is_ctx-node_key
   it_key   = it_key
  IMPORTING
   et_draft_key = DATA(draftkeys)
).

" IF the draftkeys are not initial then we proceed. This is because we
" want to create the Identification data only if the BP is being created
IF draftkeys IS NOT INITIAL.

  TRY.
    "Read the associations.
    /bobf/cl_frw_factory=>get_configuration(iv_bo_key =
          is_ctx-bo_key)->get_assoc_tab(
              IMPORTING
                et_assoc = DATA(assoctab)

```abap
          ).
     CATCH /bobf/cx_frw.
       RETURN.
     ENDTRY.
     " Get the BP Identification assiciation key
     DATA(targetnodekey) = assoctab[ assoc_key =
         zif_i_bus_parttp_c=>sc_association-zi_bus_parttp-_bpident ]-target_node_key.

     " Get the BP identification data for the current BP. The identificaiton data should only be created if it is not
     " existing. Hence only in the first call the value of bpidentifications will be empty
     io_read->retrieve_by_association( EXPORTING
                     iv_node         = is_ctx-node_key
                     it_key          = draftkeys
                     iv_association  = zif_i_bus_parttp_c=>sc_association-zi_bus_parttp-_bpident
                     iv_fill_data    = abap_true
                     IMPORTING
                     et_data         = bpidentifications ).
     " If no BP identification exists, then create a new identification
     IF lines( bpidentifications ) EQ 0.
       " Input the default values
       bp_ident_create-type            = 'FS0002'.
       bp_ident_create-entry_date      = sy-datum.
       bp_ident_create-valid_date_from = sy-datum.

          " Create the Identification data
       io_modify->create(
        EXPORTING
        iv_node           = targetnodekey
        is_data           = REF #( bp_ident_create )
        iv_assoc_key      = zif_i_bus_parttp_c=>sc_association-zi_bus_parttp-_bpident
        iv_source_node_key = is_ctx-node_key
        iv_source_key     = draftkeys[ 1 ]-key
        IMPORTING
        ev_key            = DATA(bpidentkey)
        ).

       ENDIF.

    ENDIF.
    ENDMETHOD.
```

Now let us check how this works.

Execute Transaction BOBT, open your Business Object and click on 'Add Node Instance'.

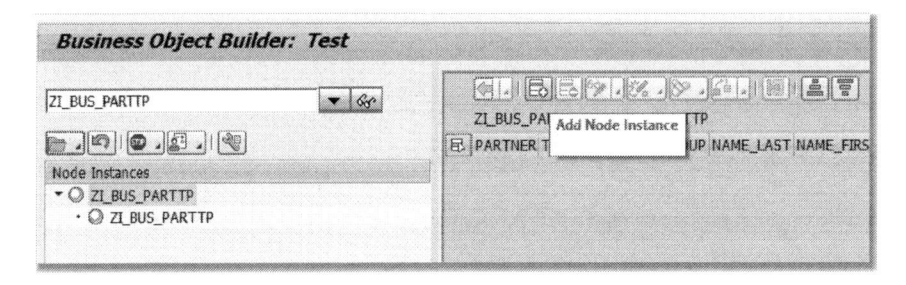

Figure 45: Create new BP data

This creates an empty line for the BP generic data.

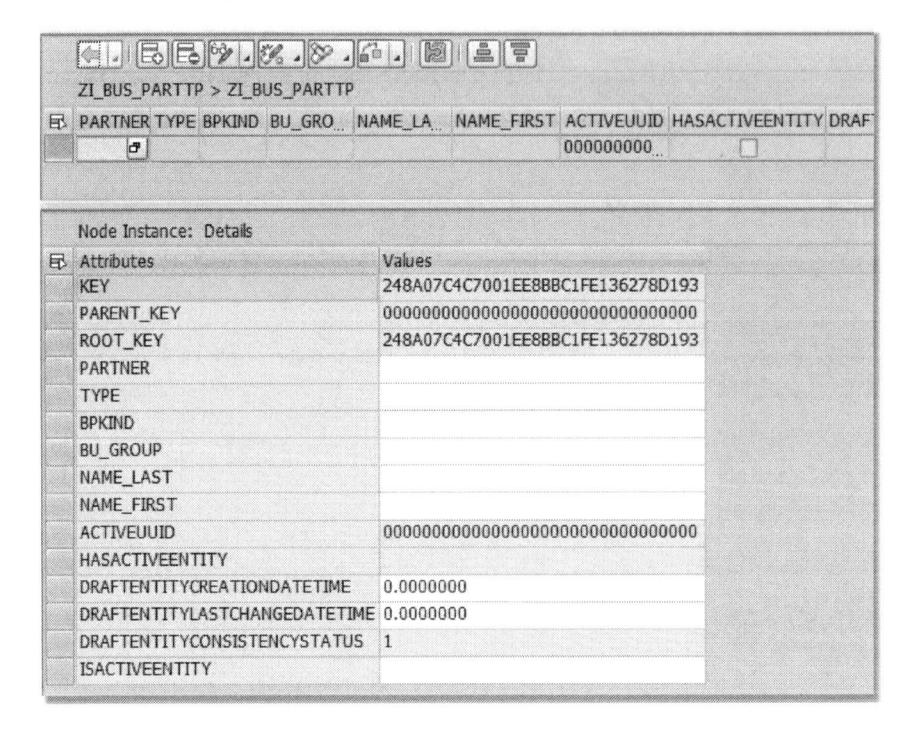

Figure 46: Enter new BP data

Now click on 'Execute Association'

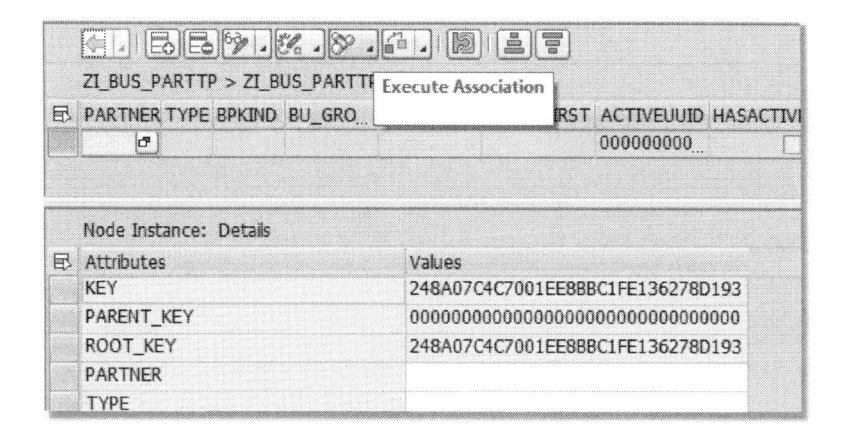

Figure 47: Execute Identification Association

You would notice that an entry for the BP Identification is already created with the default data.

Figure 48: Display Identification data create by Determination

2. Summary

As you have seen from the above steps, the new programming model simplifies the development and reduces the time to create an end-to-end application. This helps the team in focusing on the complex real-world business logic.

With this we come to the end of the exercise and hope it solves many of your queries around building a new application from scratch.

Conclusion

The chapters covered in this book took you through the key components in S/4 Hana.

Chapter 1 and 2 helped you get started with the Eclipse and New language features. Chapter 3, 4 and 5 covered he essential information required to develop applications, and finally Chapter 6 provided a detailed step-by-step guide in building a complete draft-enabled application.

Whether you are a consultant or an application developer, this book should have helped you in understanding the new programming model and will be of help in your daily work.

Finally let me 'thank you' for reading this book.

Please feel free to provide your valuable feedback by writing to me at anderson.mark.connect@gmail.com .

Also, if you need more course material or guidance then feel free to reach me.

Printed in Great Britain
by Amazon